LIVE TO DRIVE

ALI MARANDI

LIVE TO DRIVE

Dedication

To my family,
For your unwavering belief, countless sacrifices, and
endless support. Dad, your guidance and determination
fuel my drive. Mom, your love and encouragement keep me
grounded. I wouldn't be here without you both.

To my mentors,
For seeing potential in me, even when I doubted myself.
Tom and Dave, who have always been there for me. Pete,
your wisdom and patience has been my foundation.
Alessandro and Konstantin, your hard work and dedication
has shaped me into the driver I am today.

And to every fan, friend, and teammate who's stood by me,
Thank you for being part of this journey. This is for all of
you who dream big and chase it with everything you've got.

Seb

MY JOURNEY

Hi,

I'm Sebastian Eskandari, but most people just call me Seb. I'm 11 years old, and racing is my life. From the moment I first sat in a go-kart at four years old, I knew this was what I wanted to do. There's just something about the roar of the engine, the thrill of the race, and the feeling of being completely in control of a machine at speed. It's like nothing else.

This book is my story so far—how it all started, the challenges I've faced, and the people who have helped me along the way. I've raced on tracks all over Australia and even in Italy, where some of the best young drivers in the world compete. It hasn't always been easy, though. There have been tough races, tough moments, and times when I've had to dig deep to keep going.

But through it all, I've learned so much—not just about racing, but about myself. I've realized that even with talent, hard work and determination make all the difference. I've learned that setbacks are part of the journey and often lead to the biggest comebacks. Most importantly, I've discovered that when you truly love something, you find the strength to face every challenge and keep pushing forward, no matter how tough it gets.

This is my journey so far—the highs, the lows, and everything in between. It's not just about the trophies or the lap

times; it's about the passion that drives me every time I
pull on my helmet and hit the track.

I hope you enjoy reading my story. And maybe, just
maybe, it'll inspire you to chase your own dream, whatever
it might be.

Seb

Prologue

The steady roar of engines reverberated through the air, a heart-beat that pulsed through the crowd and found its way into the very core of young Sebastian Eskandari. From the moment he first wrapped his small hands around the steering wheel of his father's racing simulator, a spark had been lit. It was more than play—it was the beginning of a journey that would soon take him beyond the Australian suburbs and into the realm of fierce international competition and unwavering dreams.

Sebastian's story wasn't just about racing; it was about a fire that burned in him from the age of four, a relentless drive that propelled him forward. It was about the laughter shared with his family on sun-soaked practice days, the sting of whispered accusations that tested their resolve, and the weight of expectation as his small figure stood at the starting grid.

To the world, he was just another boy in a go-kart. But to Sebastian, each race was a proving ground—a chance to show that passion, skill, and grit could take him where few dared to dream.

This is where it all began: the sacrifices, the moments of doubt, and the victories that lifted him higher than he ever thought possible. This is the story of a young racer who set out not just to win, but to forge a path through the noise and the naysayers, driven by a simple promise—to never back down.

"THE FIRST SPARK"

The low hum of the racing simulator echoed through the living room, filling the air with the sounds of squealing tires and roaring engines. Babak sat comfortably in the driver's seat, his hands firmly gripping the wheel as he expertly navigated the track on the screen. The sharp turns ahead demanded his full attention, but out of the corner of his eye, he noticed movement.

Two-year-old Sebastian, with his fair skin, light brown hair, and wide, curious blue eyes, waddled over. Without a word, he tugged at his father's leg, his little face full of determination.

Babak glanced down, surprised but amused. "You want to drive, buddy?"

Sebastian didn't need to say anything. His bright eyes were locked on the steering wheel, and with a giggle, he reached his tiny hands up, desperate to take control. Babak chuckled, lifting him onto his lap, letting his son get a feel for the wheel. It was too big for his small hands, but Sebastian held it tightly, imitating his dad's every movement.

The car on the screen veered wildly off course, but Sebastian didn't care. He was laughing, thrilled by the rush of it all.

"Again!" Sebastian squealed, his voice bubbling with excitement.

Babak grinned, his heart swelling. There was something about the way Sebastian's eyes lit up that made him pause. This wasn't just fun for his son—it was something more. He could feel it.

From that moment on, every time Babak sat down at the simulator, Sebastian was there. It became their thing, a ritual. Sebastian would toddle over, climb onto Babak's lap, and demand to drive. He wasn't just playing. Every time he grabbed the wheel, his focus deepened, his giggles fading into concentration as the car sped around the virtual track.

By the time Sebastian turned three, Babak could tell this wasn't just a phase. His son was serious. So one day, Babak took matters into his own hands. With a bit of ingenuity and some online shopping, he put together a mini driving rig. Using Sebastian's high chair, an old gaming wheel, and some makeshift pedals that his little feet could just barely reach, Babak gave Sebastian his own simulator.

When Sebastian first sat down in his mini-rig, his face lit up like it was Christmas morning. "Dad, it's mine?"

"All yours, buddy," Babak said, ruffling his son's hair. "Let's see what you've got."

And that was it. Hours passed in a blur as Sebastian navigated the virtual tracks. The sound of engines and tires filled their Brisbane home, and the squeaky little pedals made a soft clunk each time Sebastian pushed them down with his tiny feet. It was as if nothing else existed in those moments—just the race, the turns, and the rush of speed.

Sebastian quickly learned the tracks, memorizing each twist and turn like they were part of him. His little hands would grip the wheel tighter, his eyes narrowing with focus as he tried to go faster, take the corners cleaner. Babak watched in awe. Sebastian was improving every day.

Over the next few months, Sebastian's obsession with racing had gone beyond the simulator. He would spend hours watching Formula 1, Le Mans, NASCAR—anything with fast cars. He could sit for hours, mesmerized by the speed, the skill, the drivers who seemed larger than life.

One night, after a particularly intense race on TV, Sebastian looked at his dad, his voice barely a whisper. "I want to race like them."

Babak paused, glancing at his son. He'd seen this passion build, growing stronger every day, but hearing Sebastian say it out loud hit different. It was a serious request, a moment of clarity for both of them.

"Are you sure, Seb?" Babak asked, kneeling down to meet his son's eyes. "Racing isn't just about fun. It's a lot of work, a lot of practice. It's hard."

Sebastian didn't even flinch. "I know. I want to be the fastest."

There it was again—that spark, that drive that made Babak's heart swell. This wasn't just some kid's wishful thinking. Sebastian meant it. Babak could see the determination in his son's eyes, a determination that felt far too mature for an almost four-year-old.

"Well, then," Babak said with a smile. "We'll see what we can do."

A few days later, just before Sebastian's fourth birthday, Babak decided it was time to introduce him to the real thing. He woke him up early on a Saturday morning, excitement buzzing in the air.

"Where are we going?" Sebastian asked, rubbing his eyes.

"You'll see," Babak said, trying to contain his own excitement.

They drove for what felt like forever to Sebastian, but when they finally arrived, the roar of engines greeted them, and Sebastian's tiredness disappeared in an instant. They had arrived at a small local go-kart track, and as soon as they stepped out of the car, Sebastian was transfixed.

His blue eyes widened, and his hand tightened around Babak's as they walked toward the fence. Karts zoomed by, their engines revving, tires squealing as the drivers tore around the track. The smell of gasoline hung in the air, and the roar of the engines sent a thrill through Sebastian that he couldn't describe.

His heart raced with each passing kart, his hands gripping the fence as if holding on for dear life. "Dad, look!" he yelled over the noise, pointing to a group of karts battling for position. "They're so fast!"

Babak smiled, kneeling down beside his son. "Yeah, they are. See how they take the corners? It's all about precision."

Sebastian was glued to the action. Every corner, every overtake—it was like he was on the track with them, his heart pounding in time with the karts. This was it. This was what he wanted. The feeling of speed, the challenge, the excitement—it was everything.

Later, as they walked back to the car, Sebastian's mind was still racing. He turned to Babak, his blue eyes full of determination.

"Dad, I want to do this. I want to race."

Babak stopped, looking down at his son. He had expected Sebastian to be excited by the track, but hearing him say the words out loud made everything real. This wasn't just a childhood dream. This was something deeper.

"Are you sure, Seb?" Babak asked, crouching down to meet his gaze. "It's not easy. Racing takes hard work, practice, and a lot of commitment. It's not just about having fun."

Sebastian nodded, his face set in determination. "I know. But I want to be the fastest, like the ones we see on TV."

Babak stared at his son, feeling a swell of pride. There was no doubt in his mind—Sebastian was serious about this. He wasn't just a little kid with a passing interest. He had that fire inside him, the same fire that made racers push themselves to the limit.

"Well," Babak said, standing up and ruffling his son's hair, "if you want to race, then we'll race."

Sebastian's face lit up, and Babak couldn't help but smile. He had no idea where this journey would take them, but one thing was clear—Sebastian was ready. And from that day forward, nothing would ever be the same.

The wheels of Sebastian's future were already turning.

"A KART OF HIS OWN"

Sebastian could barely contain his excitement as he rushed into the garage, his small feet tapping on the concrete floor. Babak had been acting mysterious all morning, telling him only to "wait and see." Now, the mystery sat gleaming in front of him—a real go-kart.

It wasn't new. The paint was chipped in a few places, and the seat looked like it had seen better days. But to Sebastian, it might as well have been the fastest machine in the world.

"Is that... for me?" His voice was barely above a whisper, and his wide blue eyes blinked in awe.

Babak grinned, crouching beside him. "Sure is, buddy. What do you think?"

Sebastian didn't even answer. His small hands were already running along the frame of the kart, feeling every inch of it. "It's fast," he murmured, eyes gleaming. It wasn't a question—it was a fact.

Babak watched his son with a smile. He'd found the kart online, a second-hand deal for $800, and though it wasn't perfect, he knew it was the right choice for Sebastian's first kart. But as Sebastian tried to climb in, it was obvious the kart wasn't exactly kid-sized. His feet dangled above the pedals, and the steering wheel seemed far out of reach.

Babak scratched his head. "Hm. Looks like we'll need to make a few adjustments."

Sebastian, ever determined, didn't seem discouraged. "Can you fix it, Dad?" His voice was hopeful, but his eyes were filled with trust, like he already knew the answer.

"Of course I can," Babak said, flashing a grin. "We're not giving up on this kart. I'll make it fit."

The first step was finding someone who could help. Babak contacted a go-kart shop down on the Gold Coast, explaining the modifications they needed. The shop owner had assured him they could handle it, so Babak made the drive, leaving the kart in their care.

Three weeks passed with no word. Every day, Sebastian asked, "Is it ready yet?" and every day, Babak had to shrug and say, "Not yet, buddy."

Finally, Babak called the shop. A woman answered, her voice sounding distracted. "Oh, right. Yeah. Ted said it was too hard to do. Sorry about that."

Babak's heart sank, frustration bubbling up. He hung up, grabbed his keys, and made the trip to the Gold Coast, collecting the kart that hadn't been touched. When he returned home, Sebastian was waiting, his eyes wide with anticipation.

"Well?" Sebastian asked, bouncing on his toes.

Babak sighed, but there was no way he was letting his son down. "We'll fix it ourselves," he said, determination settling in. "Come on, Seb. Let's get to work."

Sebastian's eyes lit up with excitement. "We're going to fix it? Like, really?"

Babak knelt beside the kart, laying out the tools he'd need. "You bet. We're going to make this kart fit you perfectly."

The next few days became a blur of tools, parts, and trips to Bunnings for supplies. Babak watched countless YouTube videos, learning everything he could about kart modifications. He ordered extra parts online and picked up foam padding to help adjust the seat.

"See these?" Babak said one afternoon, holding up the foam. "This will help you reach the pedals."

Sebastian watched with wide eyes, nodding as if he was learning some great secret. "That means I'll be able to drive it?"

"That's the plan." Babak grinned, and together, they worked through the small adjustments. Every evening after work, Babak would tinker with the kart while Sebastian watched eagerly, asking a million questions. It wasn't long before the kart looked ready for its first test drive.

But there was one problem—where could they safely try it out?

"Maybe we could take it down the street," Babak suggested over dinner one night.

Kelly, who had been listening quietly, crossed her arms and gave Babak the look. "Absolutely not," she said, her tone leaving no room for argument. "It's too dangerous. There are too many cars, and the concrete kerbs are unforgiving."

Babak knew better than to argue, but it was clear he'd need to find a different spot.

Early one Sunday morning, Babak found the perfect place—a quiet industrial estate in Mansfield. The roads were empty, and the wide-open space seemed safe enough for a trial run.

As they unloaded the kart, Sebastian practically bounced with excitement. His feet barely touched the ground as Babak helped him climb into the seat.

"You ready?" Babak asked, adjusting Sebastian's helmet.

Sebastian nodded, his eyes sparkling beneath the helmet's visor. "I'm ready, Daddy."

Babak crouched down beside him, resting a hand on his shoulder. "Remember, take it slow, okay? There's no rush."

"I got it," Sebastian said, his voice filled with confidence.

Babak stepped back, his heart racing a little as Sebastian pressed the gas pedal. The kart lurched forward slowly at first, and Sebastian gripped the steering wheel tightly, navigating the open space cautiously. But after a few minutes, Babak saw it—the shift in Sebastian's posture, the widening grin beneath his helmet.

He was picking up speed.

Kelly, who had been standing next to Babak with looks of concern, frowned. "He's going too fast, isn't he?" she asked, her voice edged with worry.

Babak chuckled. "I think he's just getting started."

For the next half-hour, Sebastian zoomed across the concrete, the kart weaving smoothly through the open spaces as if it had been made for him. His confidence grew with every lap, and by the time he pulled back toward his parents, his cheeks were flushed with excitement.

"That was awesome!" Sebastian jumped out of the kart, barely able to stand still. "Can we come back?"

Babak smiled, ruffling his son's hair. "Of course. Anytime you want, buddy."

But as Sebastian's speed increased, so did Babak and Kelly's concerns. The industrial estate wasn't exactly the safest place for a young driver with big dreams. After a bit of searching, Babak found a solution: Archerfield Raceway. It was a proper track, and they allowed visitors to bring their own karts on weekends.

The following Saturday, they loaded up the kart again and made the trip to Archerfield. Sebastian's excitement was through the roof as they arrived at the track. This wasn't just an empty lot—this was the real deal.

"Okay, Seb," Babak said, helping him into the kart. "This track's a little tougher than the last one. Take the turns slowly at first, and get a feel for it."

Sebastian nodded, his face serious as he tightened his grip on the wheel. "I'll go slow."

Babak couldn't help but laugh. "Right. I'll believe that when I see it."

Sebastian set off, easing into the first lap with cautious turns, just as his dad had instructed. But by the third lap, the cautious approach had melted away. He was picking up speed again, his confidence growing with every lap. By the end of the day, Sebastian was flying through the turns, his bright blue eyes focused on the track ahead, a huge grin on his face as he hit the straightaways.

"Look at him go," Babak muttered, shaking his head in disbelief.

"He's a natural," one of the track officials commented as he passed by, watching Sebastian zoom through the final lap.

When Sebastian finally pulled into the pit lane, breathless with excitement, he looked up at his dad, his face flushed and full of determination. "Can we come back again?"

"Absolutely," Babak said, his heart swelling with pride. "As often as you want."

With each visit to the track, Sebastian's skills improved, and his passion only grew stronger. Eager to see how far he could go, Babak searched for even more challenging places for Sebastian to race. That's when he discovered the track in Toowoomba.

The track was bigger, with longer straightaways and tighter turns. Babak was a little nervous at first, but Sebastian was as determined as ever.

When they arrived at the Toowoomba track, Sebastian stood in awe. "This is huge," he whispered, staring at the vast expanse of asphalt stretching out before him.

Babak knelt beside him, adjusting his helmet. "This is a big step, Seb. Take your time, learn the track. Eyes forward, okay?"

Sebastian nodded, his expression focused. "Got it."

As he climbed into the kart, Babak couldn't help but smile. This was it—the moment Sebastian had been waiting for. And from the moment he took off, Babak knew his son was ready.

Sebastian started cautiously, as always, getting a feel for the track. But after a few laps, something clicked. He began to push the kart harder, flying down the straightaways, taking the turns with precision and ease.

"He's only four?" Tom, the club president, asked, watching in disbelief.

"Yup," Babak said, unable to hide his pride. "Youngest driver you've ever had, I bet."

Tom chuckled. "That kid's got something special."

As Sebastian finished his session, he ran over to his dad, grinning from ear to ear. "That was amazing!" he said breathlessly. "I want to go even faster next time!"

Babak laughed, ruffling his son's hair. "I'm sure you will, buddy. And I'll be right here, cheering you on."

Sebastian's journey was just beginning, but Babak and Kelly already knew one thing for certain—this wasn't just a hobby for their son. This was his passion, and they couldn't wait to see where it would take him.

"FIRST RACE, FIRST LESSONS"

The hum of engines filled the air as they pulled into Greer Park International Raceway. The Toowoomba Go Kart track was alive with activity, and Sebastian could feel the excitement buzzing around him. The pit lanes were a sea of colour, karts gleaming in the sun, their bright designs hinting at speed and power. Kids in racing suits were everywhere—laughing, talking, adjusting their helmets—but they all seemed so much older, so much more experienced than he was.

Sebastian clutched his helmet tightly, his wide blue eyes darting around the track. This was his first real race. His first chance to prove himself, and even though he was only four, he already knew this wasn't just a game. This was serious.

"Hey, you ready for this?" Babak's voice cut through the noise. His dad knelt beside him, helping him strap into his gear. Sebastian nodded, his heart pounding in his chest.

"Yeah," he said, though his voice didn't sound quite as confident as he'd hoped. "I think so. But... they're all older than me."

Babak smiled softly, squeezing his shoulder. "Don't worry about them, buddy. Today's not about winning. It's about learning and having fun. Just focus on driving your best, okay?"

Sebastian nodded again, but he couldn't shake the nerves twisting in his stomach. What if he messed up? What if he wasn't fast enough? He looked around, noticing some of the older kids giving him curious glances, probably wondering what this tiny boy was doing on the starting grid.

He swallowed, gripping his helmet tighter. I'll show them I belong here, he thought, feeling a small spark of determination flicker inside him. He wasn't just here to race—he was here to prove that he could do it, no matter how small or young he was.

The official called the racers to their positions, and Sebastian found himself at the back of the grid. His kart, with its simple black and red design, looked so plain compared to the others. They were decorated in bright neon colours, sleek and polished. Even standing still, they looked fast.

He climbed into his kart, the familiar grip of the steering wheel calming his nerves just a little. This was his comfort zone. Once the engine revved, once he was moving, everything else would fade away. He'd be in control.

Babak knelt beside him again, adjusting his helmet and giving him one last look. "Just have fun out there," he said, his voice steady. "Remember, it's your first race. Learn as much as you can, and don't worry about where you finish."

Sebastian took a deep breath and nodded. "Got it."

As they rolled out for the formation lap, Sebastian felt a mix of excitement and nerves bubbling inside him. The track felt different now. It wasn't just a place to drive—it was a battlefield. The lights turned green, and suddenly, the karts shot forward with a roar, the race was on.

Sebastian pressed the gas, and the familiar rush hit him. Everything else melted away as the wind whipped around his helmet. He wove through the track, carefully taking each corner, picking up speed on the straightaways. His hands gripped the wheel tighter, his focus narrowing on the race in front of him.

The first heat felt like a blur. One minute he was at the back of the grid, the next he was weaving past a couple of karts, finding his rhythm. He wasn't sure how it happened, but by the end of the race, he'd made his way up to fifth place.

As he pulled into the pit lane, his heart was pounding, but it wasn't just from the speed—it was from the thrill. Fifth place! He couldn't stop smiling.

Babak was waiting for him, beaming with pride. "You did great, Seb!" he said, clapping him on the back. "You found your rhythm out there."

Sebastian grinned, feeling a warm glow of pride spread through him. But as they prepped for the next heat, that nervous energy returned. He glanced around at the other kids. They looked so focused, so ready. Was he really ready for this?

The second race wasn't as smooth. Right off the line, as Sebastian took the first corner, another kart bumped into him, sending him swerving off his line. His hands flew to correct the wheel, his heart leaping into his throat. For a moment, he thought he might spin out, but somehow, he managed to keep control, steering back onto the track.

But the bump had cost him. He'd lost positions, and no matter how hard he pushed, he couldn't seem to catch up. The frustration gnawed at him, but he gritted his teeth and kept going. You can do this, he told himself, trying to block out the disappointment.

The third heat was even tougher. As he sped through tree corner, another kart came too close, nearly pushing him off the track. His heart pounded as he yanked the wheel, narrowly avoiding the edge. The kart wobbled beneath him, but he managed to steady it. His nerves were on fire, but he didn't let it break him.

"Keep going, Seb!" Babak's voice rang out from the sidelines, giving him a boost of confidence. Sebastian glanced over, catching his dad's thumbs-up. I can do this, he told himself, tightening his grip on the wheel. I can still finish strong.

By the time the final race came around, Sebastian had worked his way to mid-pack. He wasn't in the top three, but he wasn't at the back either. As the race ended, he pulled into the pits, his chest heaving from the effort. He was proud, but there was a flicker of disappointment too.

One of the officials handed him a small participation medal, and Sebastian took it, giving a polite smile. He wasn't ungrateful, but the small medal didn't feel like enough. He glanced over at the podium, where three older kids stood, holding shiny trophies that gleamed in the sunlight. Sebastian's heart sank as he looked down at his medal. I wanted one of those, he thought.

Babak appeared beside him, placing a hand on his shoulder. "You did amazing, Seb. That was a tough race, and you held your own out there."

Sebastian looked up, feeling a mix of emotions. "But... I want a trophy. Not just a medal. I want to be up there," he said quietly, nodding toward the podium.

Babak knelt down so they were eye to eye. "You can get there, Seb," he said, his voice calm and reassuring. "But it takes time. Hard work. Every race is a chance to learn. Today wasn't about winning—it was about learning how to handle the challenges. Every bump, every close call... those are lessons that'll make you a better racer."

Sebastian nodded slowly, his fingers curling around the medal. He knew his dad was right. It wasn't just about speed or winning—it was about learning, improving, and handling the unexpected. And he had learned a lot today.

"Do you think I can get a trophy one day?" he asked, his voice small but hopeful.

Babak smiled, his eyes full of belief. "I know you can. If you keep practicing, stay focused, and don't give up, you'll be up there before you know it."

Sebastian took a deep breath, feeling a new determination settle inside him. He hadn't won today, but he had learned something important—he wanted this. More than anything. And he wasn't going to stop until he was the one standing on that podium.

As they packed up to leave, Babak put an arm around Sebastian's shoulders. "Proud of you, Seb. You raced like a champion today."

Sebastian smiled, glancing back at the track one last time. He might not have won a trophy today, but he knew one thing for certain—this was the start of something much bigger. He had the drive, the passion, and now, the lessons. And next time, he'd be ready for whatever the race threw at him.

"RISING THROUGH THE RANKS"

Toowoomba Kart Club had become Sebastian's second home. Every weekend, he and his family loaded up the car and headed to the track, the familiar rumble of engines already ringing in his ears before they even pulled into the lot. It was like a routine now—kart racing had become more than just a hobby. It was part of who Sebastian was.

At just four years old, Seb was the youngest driver in the Comer class. His mini chassis, fitted with a modest 80cc engine, was far from the fastest on the grid, but that only fuelled his determination. Challenges didn't discourage him—they fired him up. With his eyes locked on the track and his small hands gripping the wheel, he drove like he was holding onto his biggest dream.

Race days brought an electric energy to the track. Vibrant karts lined up, older kids adjusting their helmets and mentally preparing, faces set with the focus of seasoned racers. Seb might have been the smallest competitor, but that didn't matter to him. Confidence, he'd learned, came from within. He settled into his kart with quiet determination, his blue eyes fixed ahead, ready to take on the track.

Babak watched from the sidelines, proud but always thinking about how he could help his son improve. After that first race, where Sebastian had shown flashes of raw talent, Babak knew his son had something special. But talent alone wasn't enough. Babak wanted to give Sebastian every advantage he could, so he started searching for a coach—someone who could guide his son to the next level.

Finding that coach, however, was harder than Babak had expected. Each conversation he had ended with a polite, "He's too young," or, "Come back when he has more experience." The rejection gnawed at Babak, but he wasn't ready to give up. Seb deserved a shot, and Babak was determined to make it happen.

One afternoon, after a particularly long practice day at the track, Babak approached Tom, the club president, as the sun started to dip low over the horizon. The track was almost empty, just the hum of a few remaining karts echoing in the distance.

"Tom," Babak began, running a hand through his hair. "I've been looking for a coach for Seb, but no one will take him on. They say he's too young."

Tom scratched his chin, looking thoughtful. "You know," he said slowly, "my son Dave used to race here. He's not racing anymore, but he knows his stuff. He's been helping some of the other kids at the track... I could talk to him for you."

Babak's face lit up. "That'd be amazing, Tom. Really. I appreciate it."

The next day, Babak met Dave, and after a short conversation, Dave agreed to give it a go. "I can't promise miracles," Dave said with a shrug, "but if Sebastian's as dedicated as you say, I'm happy to help him out."

Seb took to Dave's coaching like he took to driving—with full focus. For the next two weeks, Dave worked with Sebastian, and the difference was clear right away. Dave had a way of explaining things that clicked with Sebastian. They'd walk the track together, Sebastian on his little bike with training wheels, while Dave pointed out the important spots—the best lines to take, how to approach corners, and when to make an overtake.

Sebastian listened intently, his eyes wide and focused, absorbing every word. He practiced what Dave taught him, lap after lap, getting a little better each time. His favourite part was learning how to draft, the feeling of slipping behind another kart and catching their air to gain speed. It was like discovering a secret trick.

By the end of their training, Dave was impressed. "There's something about this kid," he told Babak one afternoon, after watching Sebastian zip around the track with newfound confidence. "He's ready for his next race."

Babak beamed with pride. "I knew he had it in him."

The following weekend they were off for their second race at Toowoomba. Seb sat in the passenger seat of his dad's car, the familiar hum of the engine vibrating through the seat. Outside, the Australian landscape rolled by in a blur of greens and browns, punctuated by the occasional flash of a road sign. He adjusted the sleeves of his racing suit, the fabric worn and slightly faded from countless practice sessions. Today was different, though. Today wasn't just practice; today, he'd be competing in his second real karting race.

Beside him, Babak's eyes were focused on the road but softened as he glanced over at Seb. "Nervous?" he asked, a slight smile tugging at the corner of his lips.

Seb shook his head, but the truth was, his heart was thudding hard enough to make him dizzy. "Not really," he lied, gripping the edge of the seat until his knuckles turned white. He shifted his gaze to the road ahead, willing the nerves to settle.

Babak chuckled, seeing right through his son. "It's okay to be nervous, Seb. It means you care about this."

Seb looked down at the cracked asphalt rushing under them and took a deep breath. The words settled over him, calming him in a way that only his dad's voice could. He knew he was about to step into a world where speed, skill, and determination weren't just words—they were everything.

The kart track came into view, a loop of twists and turns carved into the earth, surrounded by an eclectic mix of old trailers, spectators, and karts humming with anticipation. Seb's pulse quickened. This was where it began.

Babak parked, and as they got out, he reached into the back seat and grabbed Seb's helmet, handing it over with a wink.

"You've got this, kiddo. Just remember what we talked about—focus, stay smooth, and keep your head in the game."

Seb nodded, cradling the helmet like it was made of glass. Around him, the buzz of engines and the chatter of drivers filled the air, but it all faded into a low hum as he took in the sight of the track. The starting line felt like a million miles away, but he knew that in a few minutes, he'd be there, waiting for the signal that would set everything in motion.

He found himself at the edge of the pit lane, watching older kids with confident strides and practiced gestures. Their laughter echoed, their movements seamless. Would he ever be that at ease? The thought gnawed at him, but he shook it away. There was no time for doubts.

As he slipped into the seat of his kart, he felt the weight of the moment press down on him. The seat was familiar but felt different now, like the start of something bigger. He adjusted the steering wheel, took a deep breath, and looked up. Babak stood at the edge of the pit, hands shoved into his pockets, eyes locked on him with an intensity that said more than words ever could.

The marshal's whistle pierced the air, signalling the drivers to line up. Seb swallowed hard and pushed the kart into position. The roar of engines filled the space around him, vibrating through the metal frame and settling deep in his chest. This was it. The starting flag lifted, and everything inside him stilled, a brief heartbeat before the chaos began.

And then, they were off.

The track blurred around Seb as he manoeuvred the kart into the first corner. The initial jolt of acceleration shocked his system, and for a moment, everything else vanished—the other drivers, the noise, even the weight of nerves. It was just him, the kart, and the track.

The engine roared as he pushed into the straight, the wind whipping past his helmet. He could feel every bump in the track through the thin frame of the kart, every vibration making him more attuned to its movements. He wasn't the fastest yet—two drivers were already pulling ahead, their karts hugging the curves with a smoothness that came from years of experience. But Seb wasn't deterred; he knew today was about learning, about showing that he deserved to be here.

He heard his dad's voice echo in his mind. *Stay smooth, stay patient.* He shifted his weight just so, leaning into the turn, and felt the tires grip the asphalt in response. The kart shot out of the curve, and Seb allowed a small smile. It felt right, more right than anything he'd done before.

A few laps in, he found himself in a tight pack, engines roaring, the sound of metal and rubber creating a symphony that raced through his veins. The driver to his left nudged him, the bump reverberating through the frame, jostling him to the side. Seb gritted his teeth, fighting to maintain control. His pulse pounded in his ears, but he steadied his hands, keeping the kart aligned. This wasn't just about speed; it was about resilience.

Out of the corner of his eye, he caught sight of Babak standing at the edge of the pit, his posture tense but unwavering. The sun glinted off his sunglasses, but even from this distance, Seb felt his dad's presence, like a silent push forward.

"Come on, Seb," he whispered to himself. "You can do this."

He tightened his grip on the wheel, pushing past the initial wave of intimidation. The next few laps were a blur of grit and determination, each turn an opportunity to push harder, every straight an invitation to catch up. He could feel the kart responding to him, almost as if it was an extension of himself. He managed to pass one driver, then another, the thrill of overtaking shooting through him like a jolt of electricity.

On the final lap, Seb was in fourth place, the podium just out of reach. His muscles ached, and sweat dripped down his temple, but he refused to let up. As he rounded the last corner, he made his move, darting into an inside line that was barely wide enough. The tires screamed as he pushed the kart, inching past the driver in third.

The chequered flag waved, and Seb crossed the finish line just ahead, claiming third place by a fraction of a second. The rush of adrenaline flooded his senses, leaving him breathless. He coasted into the pits, the roar of engines behind him fading as the world came back into focus.

Babak was there in an instant, pride etched into his expression. "Third place!" he said, eyes sparkling. "That's my boy."

Seb pulled off his helmet, a grin breaking across his face. "It felt amazing, Dad," he said, his voice hoarse from the race and the thrill.

Babak ruffled Seb's hair, the way he'd done since Seb was little. "You earned this, Seb. Every bit of it."

As the other racers filtered into the pits, Seb watched them with new eyes. Today, he wasn't just a kid dreaming about racing—he was a racer, part of this chaotic, beautiful world. And he knew, deep down, that this was just the beginning.

As the weekend unfolded, he found himself working through the field, overtaking kids who were older, taller, faster. By the time the chequered flag waved in the final, Sebastian had crossed the finish line in third place—his first-ever podium finish.

When the official called his name to stand on the podium, Sebastian hesitated. His cheeks flushed as he glanced at the small crowd watching. The other drivers seemed so comfortable up there, like they'd done it a hundred times before. But this was new to him, and suddenly, all the excitement was replaced with a wave of shyness.

"Dad," he whispered, tugging on Babak's sleeve. "Could you come with me?"

Babak smiled, understanding immediately. "Of course, buddy. Let's go get that trophy together."

Hand in hand, they walked up to the podium. As the official handed Sebastian the small trophy, he felt the weight of it in his hands. He held it high, grinning from ear to ear, his dad standing beside him. The crowd clapped politely, but in that moment, it felt like the biggest win of his life.

"Look, Dad!" Sebastian said, his voice bubbling with excitement. "I did it! I got a trophy!"

Babak chuckled, ruffling his son's hair. "You earned it, Seb. All that hard work—it's paying off."

Sebastian beamed, hugging the trophy close. This wasn't just a win. This was the first step toward something bigger. He could feel it.

As the season continued, Sebastian's skills grew. He was becoming a familiar face at the track. By the last race of the year, he'd secured his first-ever pole position on a rain-soaked track. The track was slippery, and many of the older drivers struggled to keep control, but Sebastian thrived in the chaos, navigating the wet turns with an almost unnatural ease.

After qualifying, Babak pulled him into a hug, both of them soaked but grinning from ear to ear. "Fantastic job, Seb! You're really getting the hang of this."

Sebastian grinned back, breathless with excitement. "It was tricky, but I loved it!"

From that day forward, something shifted in Sebastian. He was more driven than ever. Every spare moment he had was spent at the track, practicing his cornering, perfecting his driving, figuring out how to overtake with precision. The track became his classroom, and every lap was a new lesson.

GT PRO

44

INTRC

"BEYOND THE WHISPERS"

That first year had ended with Sebastian consistently placing in the top four, a remarkable achievement for someone so young in such a competitive field. He couldn't wait to see what the next season would bring. Turning five, Seb was no longer just holding his own—he was quickly becoming a force on the track. His skills had sharpened, his focus had deepened, and he was now consistently leading races, capturing the attention of even the older competitors and seasoned spectators alike. One by one, he began claiming victory after victory at Toowoomba, his name steadily growing in recognition among club members. It was more than skill—it was his drive, his hunger for improvement that seemed to set him apart.

By the end of the season, Seb was standing on podiums regularly, his once small and anonymous presence on the track now impossible to ignore. But with his success came new, unexpected challenges. Not everyone watching from the sidelines was impressed. Whispers started to circulate around the track, low voices carrying the kind of resentment that comes when people refuse to believe hard work could be the sole reason for such rapid improvement.

"There's no way he's that good," one father muttered after a particularly tough race. "He must have some kind of advantage."

The rumours reached Seb, as sharp as a flag snapping in a strong wind. At first, he tried to ignore them, pushing them to the back of his mind. But over time, it became harder. One afternoon, after securing yet another podium, he approached Babak, the thrill of the win dimmed by a question he couldn't shake.

"Dad," he asked quietly, tugging on his father's sleeve, "why do people think I'm cheating? I'm just trying my best." There was a vulnerability in his voice, an innocence that felt painfully misplaced in the face of such accusations.

Babak crouched down, putting a reassuring hand on Seb's shoulder. "Seb, sometimes when people see someone else succeed, they don't understand all the hard work that went into it. It's easier for them to think there's something unfair going on. But you and I both know how much effort you put into this."

Seb nodded slowly, but the sting lingered. "I just want to race. I don't understand why they have to be so mean about it."

"It's hard," Babak agreed, glancing at Kelly, who had been listening quietly. "But you can't let what other people say get to you. What matters is that you're honest, and you love what you're doing. That's what makes you a real racer."

Kelly wrapped her arms around Seb in a gentle hug, her voice soft but firm. "We're so proud of you, Seb. Don't let anyone make you feel like you don't deserve this."

Seb nodded, his mind still clouded by their words but strengthened by his family's support. He knew his parents were right, but it was hard not to feel the weight of the accusations. Even so, he knew one thing for certain: he loved racing far too much to let anyone's words hold him back.

In the weeks that followed, the whispers grew louder, becoming something darker—a small, toxic group of parents who weren't content with just muttering by the track. Soon, fake Facebook accounts and anonymous forum posts began popping up, each one laced with accusations and thinly veiled jealousy. They questioned how a kid so young could be winning so often, spinning theories that Seb and his family must be bending the rules. Every race weekend seemed to bring a fresh wave of rumours and bitterness.

Babak found himself bracing each time he opened his phone, the screen filled with messages, notifications, and forum posts questioning his son's achievements. He tried to let it roll off his back, reminding himself that success often comes with a cost, but it was exhausting. For Kelly, each new post or overheard comment was like a jab, a reminder of how unfairly their son was being judged. She knew how hard Seb worked, the endless hours of practice, the sacrifices they'd all made as a family. But to these people, his victories were just too unbelievable to be real.

One evening, after a particularly gruelling day at the track, Babak sat with Kelly at the kitchen table, his voice barely a whisper. "I don't get it. They don't see the hours we spend, the late nights, the sacrifices. They don't know how hard he works." The frustration plain on his face. "All they see is the result, and they assume there must be some shortcut."

Kelly reached out, placing a gentle hand on his arm. "We know the truth. And Seb knows it, too. That's what matters." Her voice was steady, but Babak saw the glint of sadness in her eyes. He knew this was hard for her as well.

As the online accusations persisted, Seb began to notice the tension at home. He could see it in the way his parents glanced at each other, in the quiet conversations that stopped when he walked into the room. One night, as Babak was tucking him into bed, Seb looked up with a question that had clearly been weighing on him.

"Dad," he whispered, "why do those people hate me? I've never done anything to them." His eyes were wide, the hurt evident, too heavy for someone so young.

Babak's heart twisted, and he took a deep breath, sitting down beside his son. "Seb, sometimes people have a hard time accepting someone else's success. They don't see the work, the dedication. And sometimes, it's easier for them to believe something negative instead of trying to understand the truth. It's not fair, but it happens."

Seb was silent, clutching his blanket tightly. "But I just want to race, Dad. That's all."

Babak nodded, feeling the ache in his own chest. "I know, buddy. And you're doing everything right. Those people might never understand, but that doesn't mean you should stop being who you are. Remember why you started racing in the first place—because you love it. Focus on that."

As the weeks passed, the online trolling didn't go away. In fact, they seemed to grow louder, each accusation more persistent than the last. But Seb clung to his father's words. Each time he pulled on his helmet and revved up his kart, he reminded himself that he was there for one reason: he loved racing. And no amount of jealousy or online bitterness could take that away from him.

With each race, Seb's focus sharpened. He began to view the negativity as just another challenge, something to overcome like any other obstacle on the track. He used it as fuel to motivate him. And with each podium finish, each hard-earned victory, he felt a quiet satisfaction. He didn't need to prove anything to those who doubted him. All he needed to do was keep showing up, keep giving his all, and let his actions speak louder than anyone's words.

By the season's end, Seb had not only cemented his reputation as one of the top racers at the club, but he'd also discovered a resilience he hadn't known he possessed. He learned to hold his head high, to rely on the support of his family, and to understand that success often comes with its own set of challenges. And through it all, he stayed true to the love of the sport. Because, as he reminded himself before every race, it wasn't about the trophies or the titles—it was about the pure, unfiltered joy that filled his heart every time he crossed that finish line.

"A ROLLER COASTER OF EMOTIONS AND OUTCOMES"

Sebastian sat in the backseat, watching the countryside fly by as they drove home from another race weekend. His fingers absentmindedly played with the corner of his helmet, and even though he had a win under his belt today, his thoughts kept drifting to something else. The whispers. The side glances. The way people seemed to talk just a little too quietly when he and his dad walked by.

It wasn't the racing that made his stomach knot these days. It was everything around it.

His successes on the track were undeniable. Every weekend, he came home with stories of thrilling races, of pushing his limits, of hard-won victories. But as his name grew at the club, so did the jealousy. The negativity wasn't just whispers anymore—it was starting to feel like an invisible weight every time he climbed into his kart.

Sebastian shifted in his seat, glancing at his dad, Babak, who was focused on the road, a small frown creasing his forehead. Babak had noticed the shift too. People who had once been friendly were now distant, cold even. It was the kind of thing that gnawed at you, especially when you knew it wasn't about anything you'd done wrong.

Seb's thoughts were interrupted by Babak's voice. "What's on your mind, bud?" he asked, glancing over briefly.

Sebastian shrugged. "I don't get why people are so mad at me, Dad. I'm just racing. I'm not doing anything wrong."

Babak sighed. "People get jealous, Seb. When you do well, some people don't like it. But that doesn't mean you're doing something wrong."

Seb frowned, turning back to look out the window. He wanted to believe his dad, but it still didn't make sense. Racing was supposed to be fun—about getting better, going faster, feeling the thrill of the track. Not this.

The next race weekend arrived quickly, but the tension at the track was impossible to ignore. Babak had introduced a lot of people to the club, including a family with a son just six months older than Sebastian. Their boys had started karting together, had even been friends in the early days. But now, things were different. Now, Sebastian was winning, and the other boy wasn't. What had once been friendly competition was now a source of constant tension.

Babak had enough. After another race day filled with side-eyes and hushed conversations, he found the other dad standing near the karts.

"What's going on?" Babak asked, his tone calm but firm. "Why are you spreading these rumours?"

The man folded his arms across his chest, his expression hard. "I've had experts watch Sebastian. They say it's impossible for a kid his age to come out of corners that fast. No way it's legal. I think you're modifying his engines."

Babak felt his temper flare, but he kept his voice level. "We're not doing anything illegal. Sebastian's working hard, and we've played by every rule. If you've got a problem, get the officials involved."

Despite Babak's words, the accusations lingered. Every race seemed to carry more weight than just the competition. It felt like they had something to prove now.

And then it happened. After one particularly successful race weekend, Sebastian's engine was flagged for a spot check. The main accuser stood close by, watching with narrowed eyes. Babak and Dave, Sebastian's coach, stood on the other side, trying to stay calm.

The official went over every detail, checking the engine thoroughly. After what felt like hours, the verdict came back—the engine was perfectly legal.

Babak turned to the man, raising an eyebrow. "Satisfied now? Will you leave us alone?"

But the man's expression didn't change. He just shook his head. "No. You're doing something. It's impossible for him to be that fast."

Sebastian overheard the conversation as he pulled off his helmet, his chest tightening. "Why can't they just let me race?" he thought. But instead of saying anything, he walked over to his kart, focusing on packing up his gear.

Determined to prove their honesty once and for all, Babak spoke with the club officials and requested a formal tech inspection of all the engines at the next race. "We'll put an end to this once and for all," he told Sebastian as they worked on the kart in their garage.

Sebastian didn't say much, but Babak could see the strain on his son's face. The races weren't just about the track anymore. There was a weight to every lap, every victory.

Two weeks prior to the race, Babak took the engine to Johnno, an engine builder he trusted. "They're going to inspect everything," Babak explained. "Just make sure it's perfect."

"No worries, mate," Johnno assured him. "I'll rebuild it and check everything over."

Babak breathed a little easier, knowing Johnno was on it. But when race day came, things didn't go as expected. From the moment Sebastian started his first lap, something felt off. The kart sputtered, struggling to accelerate. Sebastian gritted his teeth and did what he could, coaxing the kart around the track, but it wasn't right.

Still, through sheer skill, he managed to win the final.

As soon as the race ended, the officials conducted the tech inspection. Babak stood nearby, watching with a mix of nerves and frustration. When the results came back, the official shook his head.

"Your engine's CC is way off, Babak. It's actually so far off that it's reducing performance. I'm amazed Sebastian managed to race with it. This would've made it nearly impossible to accelerate properly."

Babak's stomach dropped. "So it didn't give him an advantage?" he asked, even though he already knew the answer.

The official nodded. "That's right. The engine would've been significantly underpowered. But since it's out of the accepted parameters, we have to disqualify him."

Sebastian walked over, his face a mix of exhaustion and confusion. "What's going on?" he asked, his voice quiet.

Babak crouched down beside him. "They're saying the engine was out of spec," he explained gently. "It didn't help you go faster, but they still have to disqualify you."

Sebastian's shoulders slumped. "But... I didn't do anything wrong."

Babak felt his heart break a little at the look on his son's face. "I know, Seb. You raced hard. This isn't your fault."

Later that day, Johnno texted Babak: "Hello my friend! Tell me about little Seb's big day out in Toowoomba?"

Babak's reply was short. "He won, but the engine failed the CC test, so he's been excluded."

Johnno responded quickly. "What…? That's rough. Call me tomorrow for a debrief."

But Babak's frustration was already boiling over. He sent one final message: "Mate, I'm angry, frustrated, and disappointed for Seb. We've lost credibility. I don't understand how an engine you rebuilt could fail. Seb's really upset. Who knows what people will say now?"

The next day, Johnno admitted that he hadn't actually checked the engine properly after rebuilding it. Babak felt betrayed. How could someone he trusted let something like this happen?

Determined to avoid any more surprises, Babak asked one of the club officials to build Sebastian's engines from then on. But things weren't smooth after that either. The official couldn't run the engines in, which meant Sebastian had to run them in during practice sessions. During one of those sessions, the engine seized up, and Babak decided enough was enough. He asked a friend to run in the engines on a dyno from then on.

But the change didn't sit well with the club official, and during the next race weekend, it became clear he wasn't happy. After Sebastian qualified on pole, they lined up for the first heat. The rain started to fall, turning the track into a slick, slippery mess. Karts spun out during the formation laps, struggling to find any grip.

Sebastian kept his kart steady, finishing third despite the tough conditions. But that night, when Babak checked the results, Sebastian was listed as a lap down.

Confused, Babak approached the official. "Why is Sebastian down a lap?" he asked.

"I issued him a one-lap penalty for going too fast on the formation lap," the official replied with a shrug.

"Where is that in the rule book?" Babak demanded. "And why weren't we notified?"

The official's answer was short. "Too late to appeal now—it's been over an hour."

Frustrated and exhausted after his conversation with the official that evening, Babak knew there was nothing he could do to change the decision. The penalty would stand. As he walked back to their trailer, the weight of it settled in. He would have to tell Sebastian in the morning.

The next day, when Babak found Sebastian already gearing up for the final race, his son's focus was unwavering. Sebastian's blue eyes were locked on the track ahead, his face set with quiet determination. Babak hesitated for a moment, not wanting to disrupt that focus, but he knew they'd have to address the penalty before the race started. Still, watching Sebastian's calm resolve, Babak couldn't help but feel a surge of pride. His son was ready, no matter what.

Sebastian started from the back, but as soon as the race began, he pushed through the field with precision, passing kart after kart. By the time he crossed the finish line, he had worked his way to first.

As Babak watched his son, he couldn't help but feel a swell of pride. No matter what they threw at him, Sebastian kept racing with heart and skill. Nothing can take that away from him, Babak thought.

Through all the ups and downs, Sebastian's love for racing endured. And while the road ahead would be filled with challenges, he knew one thing for sure—he wasn't going to stop. Not now. Not ever.

"RACING INTO NEW TERRITORY"

While Sebastian's world revolved around racing, Babak's focus had shifted. He had recently taken on the role of Vice President at Toowoomba Kart Club. For him, it was a way to give back to the sport that had already given so much to Sebastian. But stepping into the role had brought its own set of challenges.

At a recent club meeting, the tension between Babak and one of the long-time officials reached a boiling point. Babak had suggested some changes to help the club grow and improve, but the official wasn't having it.

"Everything was fine here before you and your son came along!" the official shouted, his face red with anger, before storming out of the room. The remaining committee members exchanged uncomfortable glances, stunned into silence. Babak sat there quietly, the weight of the moment settling over him. He wasn't trying to cause trouble—he just wanted to help the club, but now, it felt like he and Sebastian had become targets.

Later that evening, Babak told Kelly about the incident. "I didn't expect it to get that bad," he admitted, rubbing his temples as the stress of the day finally hit him. "It's like he doesn't even want to hear new ideas."

Kelly gave him a sympathetic look as she sipped her tea. "People don't like change, Babak. It's not about Seb—it's about them feeling threatened."

"I know," Babak said, sighing deeply. "But it doesn't make it any easier."

Sebastian, blissfully unaware of the drama surrounding his dad, sat cross-legged on the floor nearby, carefully adjusting his helmet, his mind clearly on the race ahead. His focus was always on the track, and Babak wanted to keep it that way. Sebastian didn't need to know about the frustrations going on behind the scenes. Not yet.

The following week brought even more stress when the club president received an alarming phone call from their insurance broker. Apparently, there had been a report of an underage driver—Sebastian—competing at the club, which was a violation of their insurance policy.

When the remaining committee met to discuss it, Babak was shocked. "We've been racing here for years, and no one ever mentioned this before," he said, trying to make sense of it all. "We were under the impression that the policy covered younger drivers."

The president nodded. "So was I. But now we're in a tough spot. We need to update our insurance, or we could be facing a major issue. We now have a lot of young drivers that this will effect."

That night, Babak sat at the kitchen table with his laptop, trying to figure out how to fix the problem. Kelly sat next to him, a worried look on her face. "What are we going to do?" she asked softly.

"We're going to find a solution," Babak replied, his eyes set with determination. "I'm not letting this be the reason Seb has to stop racing."

After hours of searching and countless phone calls, Babak finally found an insurance broker willing to cover younger drivers, based on how the club had been operating over the past two years. It was a huge relief, but the incident left a bitter taste in Babak's mouth. Someone had gone out of their way to try to sabotage Sebastian's chance to race, and it gnawed at him.

But now, it was time to focus on racing.

Sebastian's sixth birthday couldn't come fast enough. For months, he had been counting down the days until he was finally old enough to drive at Karting Australia tracks. He had been racing at Toowoomba for what felt like forever, but this? This was the big time. It felt like a whole new world was about to open up for him. The anticipation built up so much that it practically spilled over by the time the day arrived. Sebastian had reached the age where he could finally drive at Ipswich Kart Club. He'd also just upgraded to the more powerful Restricted Cadet 9 mini Rok engine, and he couldn't wait to test it out.

In the car ride to the track, his fingers drummed against his karting gloves as he stared out the window. Babak, his father, glanced at him with a smile. "Excited?"

Sebastian nodded, his blue eyes wide with excitement. "I can't wait! You think I'll be fast today, Dad?"

Babak chuckled softly. "I know you will, Seb. Just remember—go out there, do your best, and have fun."

Sebastian grinned, bouncing a little in his seat. The nervous energy bubbling inside him made it hard to sit still. He'd been dreaming of this day for what felt like forever, and now it was finally here.

At the track, just before his first practice, Babak and Kelly stood close by, their eyes never leaving Sebastian as he prepared. Seb's face was set with concentration, his small hands tugging on his gloves, a ritual that helped him tune out the world. As he adjusted his helmet, his mind raced with thoughts about the track, the turns, the split-second decisions he'd need to make. He wanted this to be perfect; he wanted to make his parents proud.

But behind Babak's steady gaze lay a worry he couldn't shake. He'd gotten a phone call from someone at the club a few days earlier, mentioning a letter they'd received—a letter accusing them of cheating, even before Seb had hit the track. Babak hadn't told Seb; he didn't want his son carrying that weight. But as he watched Seb now, carefully pulling on his gloves and adjusting his helmet, Babak felt the doubts gnaw at him. What if they don't see what I see? What if they never understand how hard he works? He took a deep breath, shaking off the thought. Today was Seb's day, and all Babak could do was hope that Seb felt the quiet, unbreakable belief his father had in him.

Kelly knelt beside Sebastian, gently adjusting his helmet. "You've got this, sweetie," she said with a reassuring smile. "Just go out there and have fun."

Sebastian smiled back, his blue eyes sparkling. "Thanks, Mom."

The track roared to life as Sebastian took his kart out for the first time. Babak and Kelly watched with bated breath as their son navigated the turns, hitting the straights with confidence. After a few laps, the club's junior driver coordinator gave him the nod of approval.

"He's a natural," the coordinator said with a smile. "You should be proud."

"We are," Babak replied, his chest swelling with pride. But underneath, he couldn't shake the feeling that the pressure was only just beginning.

Back at Toowoomba, Sebastian was allowed to race with his new engine, and though some people doubted his ability to handle the more powerful mini Rok, Sebastian quickly proved them wrong.

"His style, the way he slides the kart into the corners won't work with that engine," some said. "He'll struggle."

But Babak never doubted him. He watched as Sebastian not only handled the new engine, but thrived with it, continuing to win races and improve his skills.

However, new challenges arose in the form of combined Cadet 9 and Cadet 12 races. Sebastian, despite being younger, often outpaced many of the older Cadet 12 drivers. And with that success came more whispers, more accusations of cheating. The same people who had once supported him were now questioning his abilities.

One evening, after a particularly tough race, Sebastian overheard some parents making snide comments about him. He walked over to his dad, his face drawn with confusion. "Why do they keep saying we're cheating, Dad? I'm just driving like I always do."

Babak knelt down beside him, looking into his son's eyes. "Seb, some people don't understand what they can't do themselves. They get jealous. But you can't let it get to you. Focus on your driving—on what you can control. The best way to prove them wrong is to keep getting better."

Sebastian nodded, though the hurt lingered in his expression. "I will, Dad. I'll show them."

As the weeks rolled by, Babak took a big step, investing in a second-hand engine he hoped would give Seb an extra edge. He wanted his son to have every chance possible, knowing how fiercely Seb fought for each lap, each second shaved off his time. This particular race weekend, Seb would be up against Cadet 12 drivers—older kids with more experience, stronger karts, and a few inches on him in height. But Seb didn't seem fazed. If anything, he wore a quiet look of determination, eyes set on the track as he prepped himself to go head-to-head with the competition.

In the pre-final, Seb raced with laser-sharp focus, his kart practically gliding through each corner, wheels barely skimming the track as he pushed to keep up with the leaders. Babak watched, heart pounding with a mix of pride and nervousness. Each lap, Seb inched closer, eventually clinching second place with one of the fastest laps of the day. Seeing him cross the finish line, Babak could feel the joy welling up—a culmination of Seb's relentless practice, their shared sacrifices, and that unshakable belief that he could do this.

But moments after the race, just as Babak and Seb started to celebrate, an official approached them, his expression serious.

"Babak, I'm afraid we found an issue during the post-race inspection," the official said, glancing down at his clipboard. "Sebastian's engine restrictor... it's 0.05mm too big on one side."

The words hit Babak like a punch to the gut. *0.05mm.* Such a tiny margin, but enough to mean disqualification. He saw Seb's face fall, the bright glimmer of victory dimming in his son's eyes.

The official must've seen the disappointment written across their faces. "I know it's tough," he continued, offering a sympathetic nod. "This sort of thing can happen over time. The restrictor goes through heat cycles, and the metal expands and contracts. It changes size just a bit with each race. It's unlucky, but... the rules are the rules."

Seb stared at the ground, the sting of disqualification sinking in. Babak crouched beside him, placing a reassuring hand on his shoulder. "Seb, this doesn't change how you raced today. You drove brilliantly, and I couldn't be prouder," he said, his voice firm but gentle. "Sometimes, things go wrong, but it doesn't take away what you've achieved out there."

Seb nodded, his expression shifting from disappointment to resolve. Babak knew that look well. He was down, but not out.

Determined not to let the day end on a low note, Babak turned back to the official. "Would it be possible for Seb to race in the final, even if he's at the back of the grid?" he asked.

The official nodded, relieved to see they weren't giving up. Babak wasted no time. He bought a brand-new restrictor, one he measured himself to make sure it was within regulations. As he fitted the new part, Babak felt a renewed sense of purpose. This was more than a race now; it was a lesson in resilience for both of them.

Seb lined up at the very back of the grid for the final. Babak saw him take a deep breath, his shoulders straightening as he adjusted his gloves and visor. *Starting from behind wouldn't shake him,* Babak knew. Seb's focus was iron-clad, his gaze locked on the kart in front of him. Babak knew his son was ready to give it everything he had, no matter where he started.

"Just do your best, Seb," Babak said, leaning down with a reassuring smile. "You've got nothing to lose."

As the race began, Sebastian pushed his way through the pack, kart after kart. By the end, he had climbed to second place, setting the fastest lap of the day in the process.

That night, as they packed up, Babak reflected on the day's events. "I need to be more careful," he thought. "I need to check everything before each race."

It was a tough lesson, but one he knew would make them stronger in the long run.

Kelly stood beside him, watching as Sebastian laughed with his friend Zack. "It's been a roller coaster, hasn't it?" she said, her voice a mix of exhaustion and pride.

Babak nodded, smiling as he watched his son. "Yeah, but look at him. He's happy. That's all that matters."

"UNDER PRESSURE AND RISING"

Sebastian had been counting down to his seventh birthday for what felt like an eternity. Most kids might look forward to the presents or cake, but for Sebastian, turning seven meant something more—it meant he could finally race at Karting Australia tracks. This was a huge leap, a step into the big league. The excitement buzzed through the Eskandari household, but along with it came a quiet, unspoken pressure.

The morning after his birthday, the family set out for Warwick Kart Club, a two-hour drive west of Brisbane. It was Sebastian's first official Karting Australia race, and as they pulled into the track, his wide blue eyes gazed out the window, absorbing everything—the sleek karts, the serious-looking racers, the hum of engines warming up. His heart raced in time with the rumbling motors around him.

"You ready, Seb?" Babak asked, glancing in the rear-view mirror.

Sebastian's throat felt dry, but he nodded. "Yeah... I think so," he mumbled, his voice betraying his nerves.

Kelly turned around in her seat and offered him a warm, reassuring smile. "You'll do great, sweetie. Just like always."

But even though her words were meant to soothe him, Sebastian could feel the weight of the moment pressing down on his small shoulders. This wasn't like his usual races. This was bigger. As a P-plater, he'd have to start at the back of the grid behind 15 other karts, most driven by older, more experienced racers. He wasn't just racing for fun—he was racing to prove he belonged here.

While Sebastian focused on the race ahead, Babak's mind was spinning with thoughts of his own. His stomach churned with anxiety, not just for Sebastian's performance, but because of the rumours that had been circling like vultures. Every win, every podium finish seemed to stir up more accusations, more whispers that they were bending the rules. It weighed heavily on him, but he kept it all bottled up, determined not to let it show.

"Just focus on the race," Babak whispered to himself as he unloaded the kart, hoping the tightness in his chest would ease.

Sebastian climbed into his kart, gripping the steering wheel tightly. The familiar feel of the kart under him grounded him, helping some of the nerves slip away. As the race began and the engines roared to life, his heart kicked up a notch. Starting from the back was intimidating, but he wasn't going to let that stop him. He could feel the adrenaline pumping through his veins as the green flag waved, and he surged forward.

The first lap was chaotic—karts weaving around each other, engines roaring, drivers jostling for position—but Sebastian stayed calm, focusing on what he'd practiced. He darted past two karts on the first straightaway, then expertly slid around another in a corner. Each time he made a pass, the confidence grew, and the nerves melted away.

On the sidelines, Babak and Kelly stood with their eyes glued to the track. Babak's fists were clenched so tightly his knuckles had turned white, but he barely noticed. Every time Sebastian passed another kart, a small wave of relief washed over him, but the tension never fully left.

"He's doing it," Kelly whispered, almost to herself, watching their son inch closer to the front.

By the final lap, Sebastian had worked his way up to the lead. The roar of the crowd barely registered in his ears; all he could hear was the engine and the wind rushing past him as he focused on one thing—getting to the finish line. As he crossed it, the chequered flag waving high in the air, the reality of what he'd just done sank in. His first Karting Australia race, and he had won. Not just won—he'd set the fastest lap of the race too.

Sebastian climbed out of his kart, his legs shaking with exhaustion and excitement, as Babak rushed over to him, his face split into the biggest grin Sebastian had ever seen.

"You did it, Seb!" Babak beamed, wrapping his son in a tight hug. "You won!"

Sebastian blinked up at his dad, his wide blue eyes still trying to process it all. "I really did, didn't I?"

Kelly pulled him into a hug, her voice full of pride. "You were incredible out there, Seb."

It was the beginning of an incredible streak—over the next few months, Sebastian dominated at track after track, securing wins, poles, and fastest laps. But with each victory came more scrutiny, more whispers. No one seemed to believe that someone so young, so new to Karting Australia, could win that much without cutting corners.

"They've got a special exhaust," some would say. "They're treating the tires," others would mutter. "I heard he's got a communication device in his helmet," one person even claimed. It was relentless, and Babak could feel the weight of it growing with every race.

At night, Babak would lie awake, staring at the ceiling as the thoughts raced through his mind. "What if they accuse us of cheating again?" he'd think, the worry gnawing at him. "What if they disqualify Seb for something we didn't even do?"

Kelly noticed the toll it was taking on him. One evening, after tucking Sebastian into bed, she found Babak sitting quietly at the kitchen table, his head in his hands.

"Babak," she said softly, sitting down beside him. "You're doing everything right. We're not cheating, and you're making sure of that."

He sighed, his voice heavy with frustration. "I know. But it feels like no matter what we do, someone always finds something to complain about. I'm checking everything a hundred times just to prove we're not doing anything wrong."

And that's exactly what he started doing. Every race weekend, Babak would take Sebastian's kart to the tech team for a thorough inspection. He'd ask one of the other dads to check the squish of the engine, and he even had all the carburettors checked by JT, a respected engine builder. Just to be sure. Even the tires—Babak left the wrapping on them until the last possible moment, only taking them off after wheeling the kart into the out-grid before each race.

One Saturday at Ipswich Kart Club, a kind official named Maree approached Babak with a concerned look on her face. "Babak, can I ask you something? And I need you to be honest with me."

His stomach tightened. "Of course," he replied, keeping his tone calm.

Maree hesitated, then leaned in closer. "There's been talk. People are saying Sebastian has a communication device in his helmet. Is that true?"

Babak's heart sank, but he forced himself to smile. "No, Maree. I promise you, there's nothing in his helmet but his head."

Maree looked relieved but still worried. "I just had to ask."

Wanting to end the rumours for good, Babak took Sebastian's helmet to the out-grid before the race and approached Tania, another official who had always been kind to them. "Tania, could you check Seb's helmet, please? There are rumours again, and I just want to make sure we're all clear."

Tania looked confused but took the helmet anyway. "Of course, Babak. But why?"

After inspecting Seb's helmet and finding nothing amiss, Tania turned to the other drivers. "Everyone, bring your helmets forward for inspection," she announced, showing that they were keeping things fair. Her support meant the world to Seb and Babak, a reminder that not everyone was out to question their integrity.

This feeling of community extended beyond Ipswich to Toowoomba as well. Toowoomba Kart Club wasn't just a place where Seb practiced—it was where his racing journey had truly begun. For Seb, it felt like home; for Babak, it was an anchor in the often turbulent world of cadet racing. Much of that was thanks to Tom, the club president, who had become more than just a friend. He was family. Every time Babak and Seb pulled into the club, Tom was there, greeting them with a big grin and a warm welcome, his presence a source of steady support and encouragement. Tom understood the pressures of supporting a young racer better than anyone, and he'd often share his wisdom about both racing and life with Babak during their late-night chats after a long day on the track. To Babak, he was more than a friend—he was someone who'd "adopted" Seb, proudly referring to him as "my grandkid."

Tom's son, Dave, and others like Peg, Mark, the Trost's, the Hilder's, and Dynie became an unofficial family, rallying around Seb and Babak. Some weekends, Seb and his dad would stay overnight at the track, camping in their trailer. After Seb went to bed, Babak would join the others for a beer, sharing stories, laughs, and the kind of moments that lifted the weight of competition. The quiet camaraderie between them made Toowoomba feel like more than just a raceway; it felt like home.

Despite the pressure and persistent rumours, the support they had allowed Seb to thrive on the track. Later that year, he competed in the Queensland State Championships—a prestigious event drawing some of the best young racers from around the state. Seb's sights were set on first place, but he knew the competition would be fierce.

He led for most of the final, his heart pounding with every lap. But as the race wore on, Babak noticed something troubling—Sebastian's kart was losing speed. By the time he crossed the finish line, he had dropped to second place.

After the race, Babak realized what had gone wrong—the tires had gone off, and the engine had overheated, a result of his own inexperience managing the kart's performance over a long race. But even in second place, Babak and Kelly couldn't have been prouder.

"You were amazing, Seb," Babak said as he pulled his son into a hug. "I'm so proud of you."

Sebastian looked up, his face a mixture of pride and disappointment. "I wanted to win, Dad."

"I know, buddy. But second place in the state? That's incredible. You did everything right."

What eased the sting of losing was the post-race tech inspection. The engine was pulled apart and scrutinized, passing every test. Babak felt a huge weight lift off his shoulders—finally, public confirmation that they were racing clean.

As they packed up and headed home, Babak allowed himself to relax, even if just for a moment. The constant pressure, the accusations—they weren't going away. But for now, they had proof they were doing everything right. And as long as Sebastian kept racing with the passion and dedication he had always shown, Babak knew they could handle whatever came next.

"THE CHAMPION'S PROMISE"

Sebastian had been waiting for this moment for what felt like an eternity. Australia's lockdowns had been some of the strictest in the world, with months of closed tracks and restrictions that kept him away from the one place where he felt most alive: behind the wheel. The pandemic had brought the racing world to a standstill, forcing him to put aside everything he'd been working toward and leaving him restless, counting down the days until he could get back on track. The quiet streets and empty days only intensified his hunger to race again, to feel the rush of speed and the thrill of competition that he'd missed so deeply.

Now, finally, the restrictions were lifting, and the tracks were reopening. For Seb, this wasn't just about racing again—it was about seizing an opportunity he'd been denied earlier in the year. He had missed the first round of the Australian Karting Championship because he was too young. But now, with the second round on the horizon, his focus was razor-sharp. This wasn't just any race; it was the biggest of his young career, a chance to prove himself after months of lockdowns and endless practice in isolation. This race wasn't simply about competing—it was about showing his family, his rivals, and himself just how much he'd grown. It was a chance to reclaim the momentum that had been taken from him and to demonstrate, on the national stage, that he was ready for whatever challenges lay ahead.

Sitting at the kitchen table two days before the big trip to Newcastle, Sebastian twirled a fork in his hand, his blue eyes serious and focused. He glanced at his mom, Kelly, who was washing dishes by the sink. He had been thinking about this for days, rehearsing how to say it.

"Mom," Sebastian said, his voice more confident than usual, "I'm going to bring you back a trophy for your birthday."

Kelly paused, wiping her hands on a towel as she turned to face him. She could see the determination on his face, the same look he got right before a race when he'd pull on his helmet and disappear into that focused, quiet part of himself. Her heart swelled with pride.

"That would be the best birthday present I could ask for, Seb," she said, smiling as she walked over to him. She ruffled his light brown hair, leaning down to look him in the eye. "But just do your best, okay? That's all that matters."

"I will," he promised, his voice firm, almost like he was telling himself more than anyone else.

The morning of the trip came quickly. It was just Sebastian and Babak making the long drive to Newcastle. Kelly stayed home, trusting that her boys would bring back not just a trophy, but more stories of their racing adventures. The house felt oddly quiet without them, but she knew they were in good hands. They weren't alone, after all. Pitting with them were their close friends, the Trosts—Norm and his son, Luke, better known as "Turbo." The Trosts had become like family over the years, and as they all set up in the corner of the track next to a pile of old tires, it felt comforting despite the pressure that loomed over the weekend.

Babak glanced around as they unloaded the kart, noticing the other teams and their polished setups. Many of them had sleek, shiny transport trucks, rows of mechanics in matching uniforms, and drivers who had been racing at this level for years. But here they were, just him, Sebastian, and the Trosts, pitting out of their modest trailers.

"Ready, Seb?" Babak asked, adjusting the kart and checking the tires one last time.

Sebastian nodded, his face serious but calm. "Yeah, Dad. I'm ready."

Babak had learned from his past mistakes, especially from the Queensland State Championships a few months earlier. The kart had lost performance as the race went on, something Babak had taken to heart. This time, he wasn't taking any chances. He'd swapped the old wheels for magnesium ones, added an angled engine mount to improve engine cooling, and made sure everything was dialled in for the longer, more intense heats that awaited them.

"Remember, Seb," Babak said as they walked to the grid, "these kids have been racing at this level for years. It's going to be tough."

Sebastian looked up at his dad, his blue eyes filled with quiet confidence. "I know, Dad. But I'm not scared."

The words hung in the air for a moment, and Babak felt his heart swell with pride. Sebastian had a calmness about him that belied his age—an ability to focus in the moment and push through, even when things got tough.

The weekend kicked off with qualifying, and from the moment Sebastian took to the track, it was clear he was ready. The other drivers may have had more experience, but Sebastian had something else—a natural feel for the kart, an ability to navigate each turn with precision, like he and the kart were one. When the final lap ended, he had secured pole position.

As he climbed out of the kart, Babak approached him, clapping him on the back. "Well done, Seb," he said, a grin spreading across his face.

Sebastian's eyes sparkled. "One step closer to that trophy for Mom."

The next few heats were nearly flawless. Sebastian won three out of four, his kart performing like a dream. His driving was sharp, controlled, and mature beyond his years. Each time he climbed out of the kart, he seemed more confident, but still grounded—focused on the next challenge.

But despite the wins, Babak couldn't shake a growing anxiety. This was the Australian Championship. The stakes were high, and he knew that anything could happen. As he watched Sebastian line up for the final, he couldn't help but feel his stomach tighten.

"You've got this, Seb," he whispered, almost as if saying it aloud would make it true.

The final race started with a roar. Sebastian surged forward, holding his position at the front of the pack. But as the laps wore on, his main rival, a boy with years of experience and a reputation for aggressive driving, began closing the gap. Babak's heart pounded as he watched from the sidelines, his eyes glued to the track. The other boy was relentless, pushing harder with each lap, forcing Sebastian to defend his position again and again.

"You've got this, Seb," Babak whispered, watching his son navigate the pressure with a cool head.

Lap after lap, the two boys battled, each corner tighter, each straightaway faster. The tension was unbearable, but Sebastian never wavered. He had trained for this moment—each long night spent at the track, every race that had challenged him, had prepared him for this.

By the final lap, it was clear—it wasn't just about speed anymore. It was about endurance, focus, and heart. Sebastian's hands ached from gripping the wheel, and his arms felt heavy, but he wasn't going to let that stop him. He knew what he had promised his mom, and he wasn't leaving without that trophy.

As they approached the last few corners, Sebastian's rival made one final attempt to overtake. But Sebastian was ready. With a smooth, precise move, he blocked the pass and powered through to the chequered flag.

He'd done it.

Babak rushed over as Sebastian climbed out of the kart, drenched in sweat but beaming with pride.

"You did it, Seb!" Babak shouted, pulling him into a tight hug. "You are an Australian Kart Championship race winner!"

Sebastian's face lit up, his eyes wide with excitement. "We did it, Dad. I told you I'd bring home a trophy for Mom."

And that's exactly what he did. As they packed up in the fading light, Babak looked around at the other teams. They had the resources, the equipment, the experience—but Sebastian had something they couldn't buy. Grit. Determination. Heart. All the qualities that had carried him through, not just in this race, but in every challenge he'd faced so far.

The drive home felt different. There was a quiet pride in the air, a sense of accomplishment that filled the car as they made their way back to Brisbane. When they finally pulled into the driveway, Sebastian barely waited for the car to stop before jumping out and racing toward the house, the shiny trophy clutched in his hands.

"Happy birthday, Mom!" he exclaimed, holding the trophy out in front of him like a prized gift.

Kelly knelt down, pulling him into a tight hug, her eyes glistening with tears. "It's perfect, Seb. I'm so proud of you."

And as Babak stood there, watching his son beam with pride, he knew that this was only the beginning. Sebastian had won at the highest level, but there would be more races, more challenges.

For now, though, they could savour the victory—one that came from heart, hard work, and a promise fulfilled.

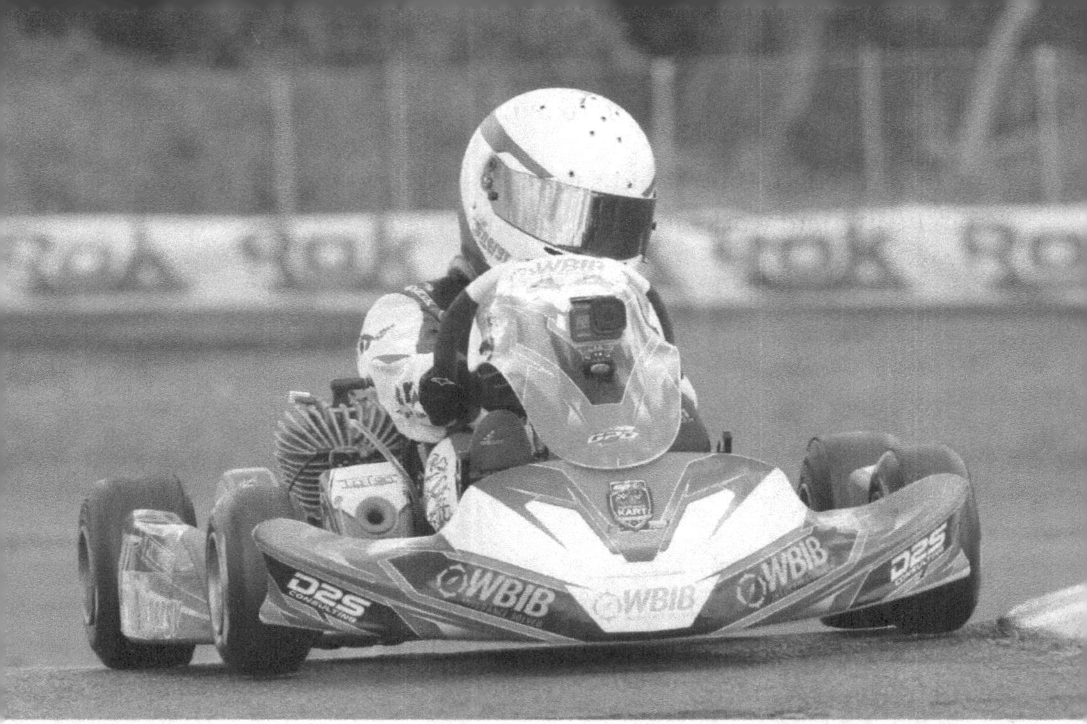
WBIB
WBIB
WBIB
D2S CONSULTING
D2S

SP tools
AUSTRALIAN
KART
CHAMPIONSHIP
USTRALIAN
KART
AMPIONSHIP
sparco
Energy

DUNLOP
KARTSPORT
sparco

KAR
OMP

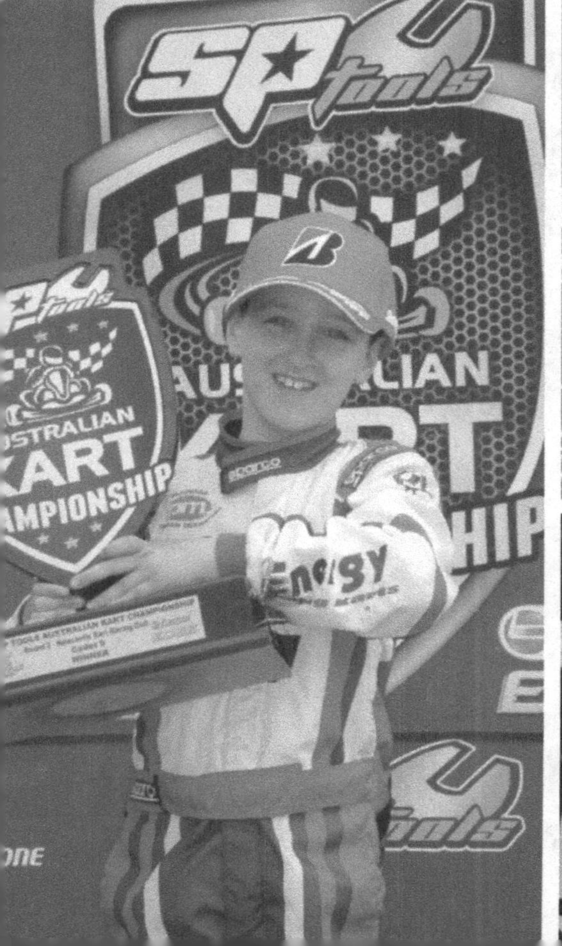

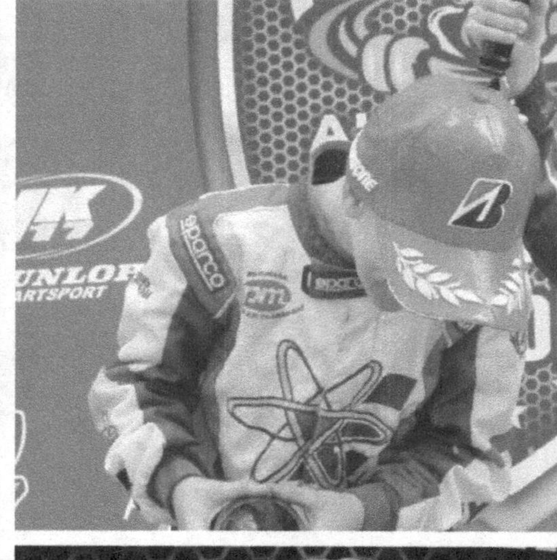

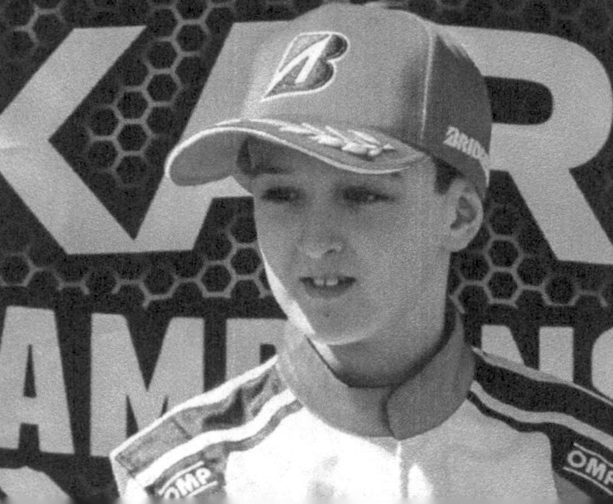

"THE CHAMPIONSHIP YEAR"

The 2021 Australian Kart Championship was a fresh start—a long-awaited chance for Seb to compete in a full season after the interruptions and frustrations of the previous year. Further lockdowns following the Newcastle round had cut the 2020 championship short after just two rounds, leaving Seb with an unfulfilled hunger to prove himself. He had spent those months practicing whenever restrictions allowed, sharpening his skills and preparing for the moment he could get back on the track. Now, with the championship returning and a complete four-round series ahead, the stakes felt higher than ever. Adding to the excitement, Seb had joined the Parolin team, a step up that came with new expectations and the chance to race under one of the most respected banners in karting. It was finally his time, and he was determined to make the most of it.

Seb's home track, Ipswich Kart Club, hosted the first round. Seb could have driven the track in his sleep, but familiarity didn't make the stakes any lower. He climbed into his kart for qualifying, the scent of rubber on asphalt filled the air. The sun casting a golden hue over the track he'd driven on countless times before. He glanced toward Babak and Kelly, who stood near the fence. Their presence steadied him.

"You know this track," Seb told himself. "Just do what you've done a hundred times before."

Seb gripped the wheel tighter. The kart hummed beneath him as he rolled onto the circuit, his focus narrowing to the track ahead. Lap after lap, he pushed harder, finding the perfect lines. When the session ended, he'd secured pole position.

"Good job, mate!" Babak said, clapping him on the shoulder as Seb climbed out of the kart.

Seb grinned, but his eyes flickered to the sky, where dark clouds loomed. "Looks like rain."

And rain it did. By the time Heat 1 began, the track was slick, and the team had gambled on a setup that wasn't quite right. Seb fought hard, but he couldn't stop the kart from sliding in the corners. He crossed the line in fifth, frustrated but determined.

Back in the pits, Babak crouched by the kart, his hands busy adjusting the setup. "It's one heat, mate," he said calmly. "Let's focus on the next one."

Seb nodded, pushing the disappointment aside. Over the next three heats and into the final, he unleashed the full force of his talent. His lines were sharp, his overtakes precise, and his focus unwavering. In the final, he broke away from the pack, crossing the finish line over two seconds ahead of his nearest competitor.

Seb's first full season in the Australian Kart Championship was off to a flying start.

The second round at Todd Rd in Melbourne brought new challenges. Seb qualified second, narrowly missing pole, but his confidence was unshaken. The first two heats saw him drive with a mix of aggression and control, taking back-to-back wins. His kart felt like an extension of himself, responding to every nudge and twist of the wheel.

Seb felt unstoppable—until Heat 3. Rain had left the track damp. After a long discussion, Seb and the team decided to gamble on slicks, despite everyone else electing to use wets, hoping the track would dry quickly. It didn't. Seb felt the kart sliding out from under him on every turn. No matter how hard he fought, he couldn't keep up, finishing 17th.

In the pits, he pulled off his helmet, his amusement clear. With a small grin on his face "Well that was a disaster. Maybe slicks wasn't the best decision," he muttered.

"It was a gamble," Babak said, crouching beside him. "And sometimes gambles don't pay off. What matters is how you bounce back."

Heat 4 gave him the chance to do just that. Starting from P6, he clawed his way back to third, setting himself up for a strong final. When the green flag waved, Seb launched off the grid, moving into second by the end of the first lap. On lap two, he seized his opportunity, diving into the lead with a decisive move. He crossed the finish line over 1.5 seconds ahead, his confidence restored.

As he climbed out of the kart, Babak was waiting. "That's what I'm talking about," he said, pulling Seb into a quick hug.

Seb grinned. "I told you I had this."

Round 3 took the championship to Bolivar in South Australia. Seb arrived with quiet confidence, bolstered by his recent success. The track was technical and tight, rewarding precision and patience—skills Seb had honed over the years. He claimed pole position with a blistering lap and went on to dominate the weekend. Heat after heat, he led the field, never looking back.

In the final, Seb was untouchable. His lines were perfect, his speed relentless. As the laps ticked down, the gap between him and the second-place driver grew to over eight seconds. When Seb crossed the finish line, he threw his arms into the air, the sheer exhilaration of a flawless performance washing over him. This wasn't just a win; it was a statement. At only eight years old, he had secured his place as the youngest Cadet 9 Australian Kart Championship winner in history—and there was still one round to go.

The final round at Monarto held the promise of a fairy tale ending. Seb entered the weekend as champion-elect, his points lead unassailable. But he wasn't content to cruise—he wanted a perfect round to cap off the season.

Qualifying set the stage. Seb's lap was flawless, putting him on pole by half a second. In the heats, he was unstoppable, winning each race by margins of over four seconds. By Sunday afternoon,

Seb lined up for the final with one goal: to make it a clean sweep for the round and the year.

As the green flag waved, Seb launched off the line, his kart darting toward the first corner. But then, disaster struck. P3 collided with the back of Seb's kart, spinning him around. He fought to restart the engine, his hands trembling with frustration as the pack disappeared into the distance.

"Come on, come on," he muttered, the engine finally roaring to life.

He re-joined the race dead last, his mind racing as fast as his kart. "Focus," he told himself. "You've got time. Just take it one lap at a time."

The fightback began. Lap by lap, Seb chipped away at the field, his focus razor-sharp. He weaved through traffic, finding gaps where there seemed to be none. By the final lap, he had clawed his way back to P6, setting the fastest lap of the race in the process. It wasn't the ending he'd envisioned, but it was a testament to his grit and determination.

As Seb pulled into the pits, the roar of engines fading behind him, Babak was already there, waiting with open arms. He rushed toward his son, pride radiating from every step.

"That was incredible, Seb," Babak said, pulling him into a tight hug. "You never gave up. That's what makes a champion."

Seb nodded, his chest heaving as he tried to steady his breath. "I did my best," he admitted, his voice quiet but tinged with determination.

"You did," Babak said firmly, stepping back to meet his son's gaze. "You did amazing, the way you fought back. You showed heart. That's what truly matters."

As Babak's words sank in, Seb noticed a flurry of movement near the kart. The Parolin team, with proud smiles on their faces, were holding out something that made Seb's heart skip a beat—a green number one plate. The iconic marker of a champion, ready for him to stick onto his kart.

"Come on, champ," one of the mechanics called, waving Seb over. "This is yours."

Seb's exhaustion melted into excitement as he made his way to the team. Together, they gathered around the kart, the atmosphere buzzing with celebration. With a firm hand and a huge grin, Seb pressed the green number one plate onto his kart, its bold presence solidifying his incredible achievement.

The team erupted into cheers, pats on the back, and even a few whistles. Seb looked around at the faces of his team, his family, and the kart that had carried him through every battle.

In that moment, surrounded by their unwavering support, Seb wasn't thinking about the challenges of the final or the what-ifs of the race. All he felt was gratitude and pride—a young champion standing at the start of something even bigger.

As Seb stood by the track, watching the sun dip below the horizon, he reflected on the season. It had been more than just a championship. It was a journey of growth, resilience, and triumph. The trophies and titles were proof of his progress, but the lessons learned—the ability to push through setbacks, to focus on the next lap instead of the last—were what truly defined his year.

"THE TURNING POINT"

Sebastian sat cross-legged on the floor of his family's trailer, the trophy still nestled in his lap. The bright green number one on the plate caught the last of the day's sunlight, and for the first time since the race ended, the weight of it all hit him. Australian Cadet 9 Champion. It wasn't just the physical weight of the trophy. It was the culmination of a year filled with long days at the track, the highs of winning, and the lows of disappointment.

His mom, Kelly, was watching him with one of those warm smiles she reserved for moments like this—moments where words weren't necessary because she could see everything on his face.

"You really did it, Seb," she said softly, stepping closer and kneeling down beside him. She placed a hand on his shoulder, gentle but grounding. "How do you feel?"

Sebastian didn't answer immediately. He stared at the reflection in the trophy, the polished gold reflecting the sun back at him. He'd seen it there all day, the proof that he had won. He looked at his mom, his voice barely above a whisper.

"I feel… good. I worked really hard for this, Mom."

And it was true. Every late-night kart prep session with his dad, every lap he'd pushed himself to shave off a fraction of a second, every ounce of effort poured into his racing had led to this moment. His father, Babak, joined them, crouching down beside Sebastian and placing a hand on his other shoulder.

"You earned every bit of it," Babak said, his voice filled with the quiet pride of a father who had been there through every step of the journey. "But now, we're looking ahead."

Sebastian nodded. He knew what "ahead" meant: Cadet 12. It was the next big step, the place where drivers between 10 and 12 years old raced. But Sebastian wasn't 10. He had just turned 8, but Karting Australia had granted him special permission to race in Cadet 12 early—which would make him the youngest ever to compete in the class. And while he felt proud of that, he also felt the pressure building.

The next season would be harder, and his dad knew that. Babak was always careful not to push too hard. "You will be racing against older kids next year, Seb," he reminded him as they packed up the trailer. "Just do your best and remember to stay calm. The races will be tougher."

Sebastian tightened his grip on the trophy, looking up at his dad. "I know, Dad," he said, his voice steady. "But I'm ready. I can feel it."

And he was ready. The following year, when the Australian Kart Championship season began in the Cadet 12 class, Sebastian felt a different kind of energy. The nerves were still there, that familiar twist in his stomach before a race, but so was the excitement. This was a new challenge, and Sebastian loved challenges.

Before his first qualifying session, he adjusted his helmet, staring down at the kart that had been meticulously prepared by his dad. Every part of it was tuned to perfection, and now it was up to him. "I'm ready," he told himself as he climbed into the seat. The weight of the kart, the feel of the steering wheel in his hands—it felt right.

Babak leaned down, checking the kart one last time, and met his son's eyes. "You've got this, Seb. Just focus on your lines."

Sebastian nodded, but the nerves were there. "I know. I'll do my best."

As the session started, that familiar surge of adrenaline washed over Seb, but he took a steadying breath, holding his focus. *Keep it together,* he reminded himself, gripping the steering wheel tighter as he entered the first few corners. These drivers were fast—faster than anything he'd faced in Cadet 9—but he wasn't about to let that get to him. Each corner was a chance to find his rhythm, to dial into the track. He repeated it in his head like a mantra: *Focus on the corners, hit your marks.*

But then disaster struck. On the fast left-hander, his cold tires couldn't grip the cold track, and the kart jerked into a massive understeer. His heart leapt into his throat as he veered off-course, his mind racing. Instinct took over as he steered down the escape road, narrowly avoiding a spin. Taking a shaky breath, he quickly turned the kart back around and re-joined the track, forcing himself to refocus. *You've got this, Seb. Just stay steady,* he thought, shaking off the slip-up.

With only four minutes left, he felt the pressure mount, but the fire to prove himself burned brighter. He slowly began pushing the limits, lap by lap, and as the tires warmed up, the kart transformed beneath him. It clung to the track like it was on rails, responding to his every move, faster and more precise with each turn. The kart felt alive, like they were working as one.

When the session ended, Seb crossed the finish line with the fastest lap. He had secured pole position—the youngest ever to do so in Cadet 12. As he rolled past the fence, he spotted his mom, her face lit up as she held up her finger, signalling "number one." A wave of disbelief and pride hit him. "I did it," he whispered to himself, his heart soaring.

As he climbed out of the kart, his dad was there in an instant, his face beaming with pride. And then his mom wrapped him in a tight hug, her joy contagious. In that moment, Seb knew he'd earned every bit of it—the long days, the endless laps, the nerves. Today, he felt unstoppable.

"You did it, Seb," Babak said, his voice calm but filled with pride. "You stayed focused and drove smart, and that's what counts."

Sebastian barely heard him. His mind was still racing, thinking about every corner, every lap, how the kart felt. He had done it, he had secured his first cadet 12 pole, but he knew it was only the beginning.

The rest of the weekend felt like a whirlwind of races, one after the other. Sebastian secured multiple fastest laps, proving that he wasn't just some kid lucky enough to get into Cadet 12 early—he belonged there. His confidence grew with every race, but so did the pressure.

After the pre-final, after Sebastian had won by a significant margin, Jimmy, the engine builder, pulled Babak aside. Sebastian saw them talking, their heads bent together in quiet conversation. It wasn't unusual for his dad to talk strategy with the mechanics, but there was something different about this conversation.

Later, as they prepared for the final, Babak approached Sebastian, his face serious. "Jimmy said we might need to slow you down a bit," he said quietly, glancing at the other teams milling around. "You're winning by too much."

Sebastian frowned. "Slow me down? Why?"

"People are talking," Babak explained, his voice calm but with a hint of tension. "Jimmy says we don't want too much attention, especially with engine claiming."

Sebastian had heard of engine claiming, a rule that allowed other competitors to buy your engine at retail price if you placed in the top three. If you refused, you'd lose all your points for the round. The thought of someone taking his engine—something he had worked so hard to perfect with his dad—made his stomach twist.

"Let's just be smart about this," Babak continued. "We're not slowing you down, but we'll figure something out."

In the end, the decision was made to use a practice engine for the final. It wasn't as fast as the race engine, but it would avoid any issues with engine claiming. Sebastian understood why they had to make the switch, but as he sat in his kart waiting for the green flag to drop, the doubt started to creep in.

"What if it's not fast enough?" he thought, gripping the steering wheel tighter. "What if I can't hold them off?"

Riley, one of the toughest competitors in the Cadet 12 class, was lined up right behind him, and Sebastian could feel the pressure. From the moment the race started, Riley was there, pushing him harder than anyone else had.

"Just keep calm," Sebastian told himself, trying to focus on the track ahead. "You know how to race. You can handle this."

But with two laps to go, Riley made his move, passing Sebastian on the inside. For a brief moment, panic flared in Sebastian's chest. "He got me," he thought, the realization hitting him hard. "What do I do now?"

But then, just as quickly, the panic disappeared. "I can get him back," Sebastian told himself, his heart racing but his mind sharp. "I just need to wait for the right moment."

On the final lap, as they approached the last few corners, Sebastian saw his chance. Riley was leaving just enough space on the outside, and Sebastian took it. With a perfectly timed move, he passed Riley, holding him off until the chequered flag waved.

As soon as he crossed the line, Sebastian let out a breath he didn't even realize he'd been holding. The relief, the excitement, the exhaustion—it all hit him at once.

"You did it, Seb!" Babak yelled, running over from the infield. He pulled Sebastian into a hug, his voice thick with emotion. "You really dug deep for that one."

Sebastian wiped the sweat from his face, still catching his breath. "It was tough, Dad. But I wasn't going to give up."

The rest of the season continued much the same way. Sebastian secured more poles, more wins, and by the penultimate round, he had already earned enough points to be declared champion-elect. The youngest ever to win back-to-back Australian Kart Championships, first in Cadet 9, and now in Cadet 12. It was a moment to be proud of, but Sebastian didn't let it get to his head. He still had one more race weekend ahead.

The final round of the season was at Newcastle, and right away, Sebastian could feel something was wrong. The kart wasn't performing like it had in previous rounds. He was losing speed, especially on the straights, and no matter how well he drove through the corners, the kart just wasn't giving him what he needed.

"Why is it so slow?" Sebastian thought, frustration building as he struggled to keep up. Even though he managed to qualify second, the speed difference was too noticeable to ignore. He was losing 7-8 km/h down the straights, and by the time the final race came, he knew he'd have to rely on strategy to get through.

"Just focus on the start," he told himself, sitting in the kart before the green flag dropped. "You can make up for the speed in the corners."

And he did. Although the kart wasn't performing at its best, Sebastian drove smart, making the most of every corner, every braking zone, every opportunity. When the race ended, he crossed the line in fourth place.

After the race, Babak walked over to the fence where the engine builder stood, Jimmy's face a mixture of exhaustion and apology. "What happened with the speed today?" Babak asked, though he already knew the answer.

Jimmy sighed, shaking his head. "Sorry, mate. We just didn't have it today."

Babak nodded, accepting the answer. "We'll figure it out."

Despite the setback, the championship was theirs. At just nine years old, Sebastian had etched his name into the history books as the youngest Cadet 12 Australian Karting Champion. Not only that, but he had also achieved the extraordinary feat of becoming the first back-to-back Australian Karting Champion across the cadet classes. Yet, as the sun dipped below the horizon and the hum of the paddock began to quiet, Sebastian wasn't focused on the win. As they packed up the kart and loaded the trailer, his mind was already racing ahead, fuelled by a mixture of determination and curiosity. The journey so far had been remarkable, but deep down, Sebastian knew that this was just the beginning. The question wasn't about what he'd achieved—it was about what came next.

CPAROLIN
44

2021 AUSTRALIAN
KART CHAMPIONSHIP
1

CPAROLIN
50

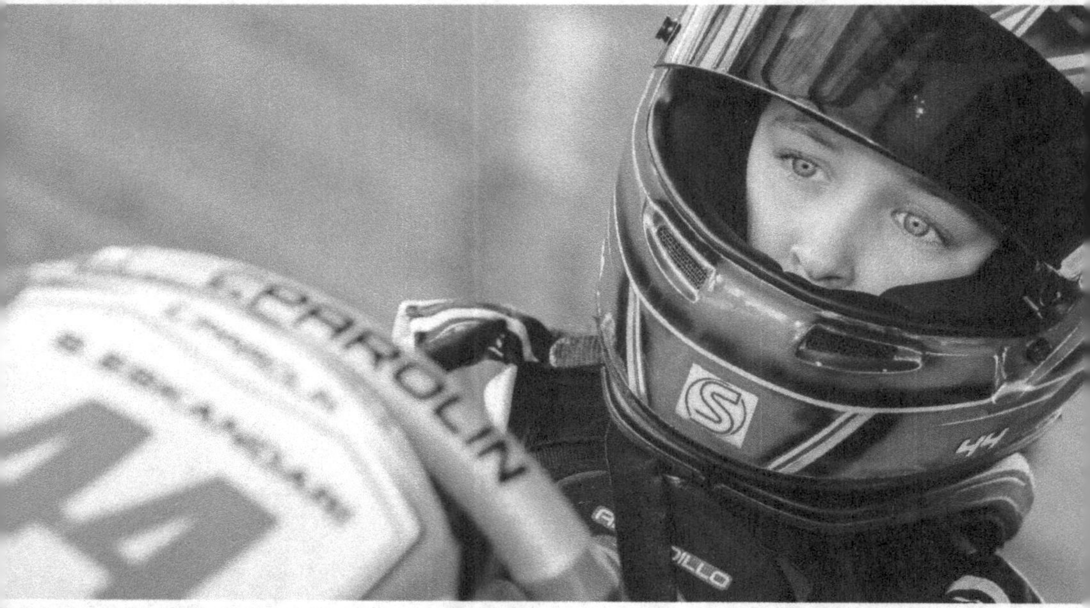

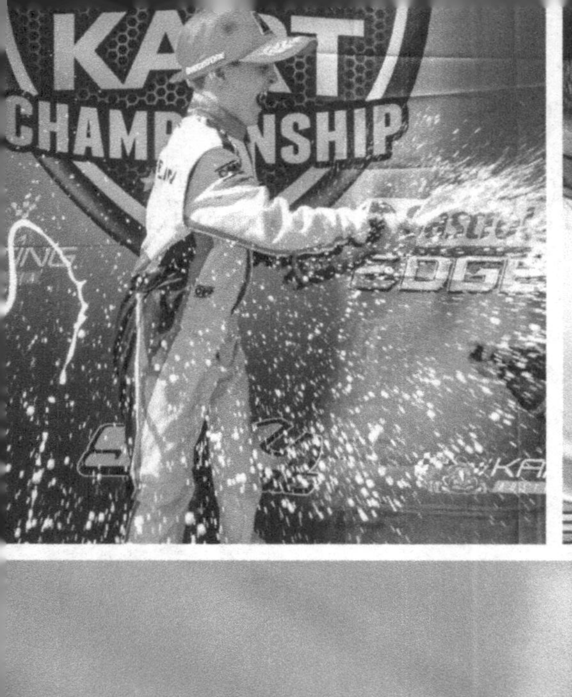

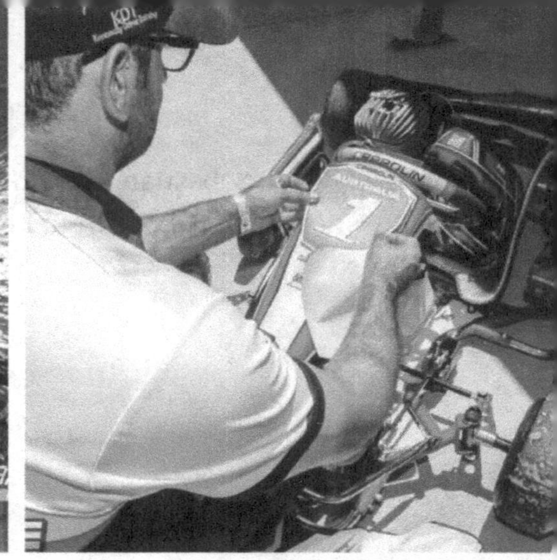

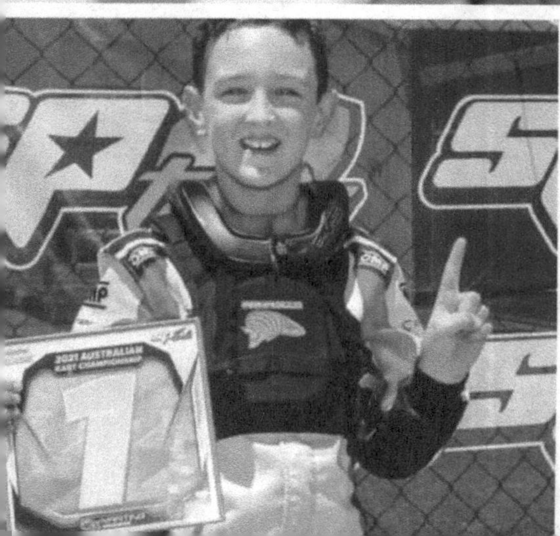

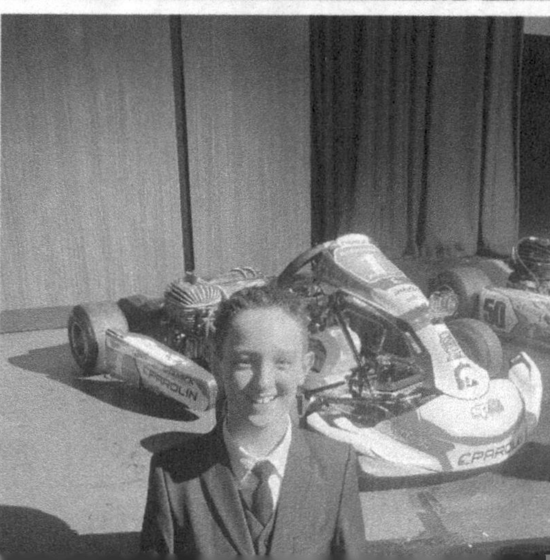

"BREAKING AWAY"

The following month, Seb found himself back at Newcastle, gearing up for the New South Wales State Championship. This time, Babak had made the tough call— they decided to race outside of the Parolin team, choosing instead to pit with friends and to use a different engine builder after the issues they'd faced in the last round of the Australian Championship. The decision was a statement, and it hadn't gone unnoticed. The Parolin team manager, who'd once championed their victories, confronted Babak the evening before the weekend started.

"You can't do this," the manager's voice was sharp, cutting through the night air of the paddock. "It's not up to you."

Babak stood there, his posture tense as the Parolin team manager loomed close, anger radiating from him.

"You can't just walk away!" the manager shouted, his voice harsh and unyielding. He jabbed a finger in Babak's direction, eyes narrowed with frustration. "You're making a mistake that'll ruin everything for him."

Babak's expression was set, the lines on his face deepening as he took a breath to steady himself. "I'm doing what's best for Sebastian," he said firmly, his voice calm but unyielding.

The manager's face flushed red, his voice rising with each word. "Best for him? Do you really think racing without us is the right move? You're ruining your kid's career."

For a moment, Babak felt the sting of the words, the weight of the accusation settling in his chest. He glanced briefly at the horizon, the sky darkening as if mirroring the storm between them. He stepped back, deciding that any more words would only fan the flames. Without looking back, he turned and walked away, leaving the manager shouting after him, "You'll regret this, Babak. Remember that!"

As Babak stood alone in their tent, the weight of the weekend pressed down on him. The risk was real, but so was the determination driving him forward.

The next morning, Sebastian stepped into the paddock, the energy of race day buzzing in the crisp morning air. He caught sight of his dad across the way and lifted a hand in a quick wave. Babak returned the gesture, a flicker of worry shadowing his eyes, a silent reminder of the confrontation that had unravelled the night before. Seb remained blissfully unaware, his focus already zeroed in on the day ahead. This weekend was going to test them in ways neither of them could predict, and Babak could only hope they were prepared for it.

The morning's tension melted into the hum of engines and the clamour of the track as the race weekend unfolded. With a strong qualifying session and impressive heat results behind him, Sunday brought a surge of confidence. Seb had just crossed the finish line in the pre-final, a victorious grin hidden behind his visor as he navigated his kart back to the pits. The rumble of the engine still thumped in his chest, the rush of triumph warm and intoxicating as he slipped off his gloves.

The afternoon came, and the final loomed closer. The atmosphere in the pits was frenetic—wrenches clinking, engines revving, the scent of fuel thick in the air. Sebastian slipped on his gloves, flexing his fingers as he ran through his mental checklist. Babak was beside him, eyes narrowed with that look he always had when something wasn't quite right.

Suddenly, Babak's brow furrowed deeper. "Seb, hold up," he said, crouching next to the kart and inspecting the brake assembly. "This doesn't feel right."

Sebastian's stomach dropped as he knelt down beside his dad. The brake master cylinder was glistening with a tell-tale sheen of leaking brake fluid. The seals in the master cylinder had given way. A knot of dread twisted in his chest. This was more than just a minor setback—this was a race-stopper.

"We can't go out like this," Babak muttered, the urgency in his voice barely masked.

Seb glanced around, the buzz of the pits blurring into background noise. The other drivers were making final adjustments, their teams crowded around them, laughter and chatter filtering through the tension. But here, in their corner, everything felt like it was teetering on a knife's edge.

"Pete!" Babak called out. Peter came over, wiping his hands on a rag, eyebrows raised

"What's going on?"

"It's the brakes," Babak said. "Calliper seals are done. We need a miracle. There is no way we can replace them in time."

Just then, Damian Folley, a friend who had been watching the commotion, stepped forward. Damian was the kind of guy who was always there to lend a hand. There had been numerous times in the past that he had got Seb and Babak out of 'mechanical' jams. "Damo, the brake seals are gone. There is no brake pressure!"

Without hesitation, Damian's face lit up with an idea. "I've got my son's brake system in the trailer. It's yours if you need it."

Seb's eyes widened, hope flickering. "Really? Are you sure?"

"Absolutely," Damian said, already moving towards his trailer. "Let's get you back out there."

The minutes that followed were a blur. The clatter of tools, the hum of voices, the swift and practiced movements of hands switching out parts, as their friends Peter and Patrick swapped the brake system over. Sebastian stood by, hands clenched, heart pounding so hard it felt like it would break free from his chest. He met Babak's eyes, searching for reassurance.

"We've got this, Seb," Babak said, a rare, soft smile breaking through the stress. "You're going to race."

As the last bolts were tightened and the brake system clicked into place, Seb exhaled a shaky breath. The roar of the engines on the starting grid called to him, and for a moment, everything else fell away. They rushed to the out-grid. He nodded to Babak and slid into his kart, the weight of the past few days settling over him like a cloak. It was time to race, and no matter what, he knew they'd done everything they could to get him here.

The final race blurred past in a rush of adrenaline and intense focus. Seb felt the kart roar beneath him, each vibration and turn grounding him in the fight he was determined to finish. Every lap, he pushed harder, gripping the wheel, his mind calculating every move—timing the brakes, perfecting the corners, finding just the right lines.

With each lap, his confidence grew, his body moving instinctively with the kart. The brakes held steady, allowing him to press forward, closing in on the pack. He managed to work his way into third place, and as the chequered flag waved, a mix of relief and quiet pride settled over him. They had made it through the struggle, holding their ground till the end. They hadn't won, but they had salvaged something out of chaos.

As they packed up that evening, the glow of the track lights casting long shadows across the asphalt, Babak stood a moment longer, watching Seb laugh with Damian. The relief of the day was tinged with a quiet resolution. "This is it," Babak thought, eyes narrowing. "No more racing with Parolin in Australia."

Seb's journey, however, was far from over. His success in Cadet 12 had opened doors that once felt like dreams—an invitation to the World Rok Cup Final at South Garda in Italy. It was a chance to compete with the best, to stand at the start line on the world stage. But after what had happened in Newcastle, Babak knew they needed a change.

Seb was set to race with the Polish Parolin Team, followed by a two race series, the WSK Final Cup with the factory Parolin Team. A plan Babak had carefully put into motion months ago. The excitement should have been enough to ease the tension that had been simmering under the surface, but that evening, as Seb dozed off in the small hotel room, Babak sat at the small wooden desk, his laptop casting a pale glow over his tired face. The room was quiet except for the soft rhythm of Seb's breathing. Babak's fingers hovered over the keyboard, the weight of the season pressing heavily on him.

Is this the right move? he wondered, glancing over at his son, whose face was peaceful in sleep. Memories of races filled with frustration, of whispered accusations and hard-fought podiums, stirred in Babak's chest. They needed a change. Something that would set Seb on a path where he could thrive, away from the shadows that had started to gather.

With a deep breath, he began typing a message to Parolin, the words coming slower than usual. He expressed his gratitude—the good races, the experiences, the growth—but there was no room for hesitation. He ended the message with a firm note: they were moving on, they will not be racing the WSK Final Cup with them. His heart clenched as he hit send, the weight of finality settling over him.

The silence felt louder after that, broken only by the soft clicks of the keys as he reached out to his friend, Peter Quintiliani. "Can you arrange a test with the Tony Kart team in Italy?" he wrote, his pulse picking up speed. A new chapter needed to begin, one where Seb could push forward, unhindered by the past.

Babak shut the laptop and rubbed his eyes. He looked at Seb again, a small smile breaking through his exhaustion. *This is for you, son,* he thought. *For all the dreams you're racing toward.*

"A DREAM UNFOLDS"

The sky over Italy was a deep blue, cloudless, and crisp as Sebastian peered out of the airplane window, watching the endless stretch of land below. His heart pounded in sync with the hum of the engine, a mix of excitement and nerves swirling inside him. This wasn't just another race—it was his first international competition, and the weight of it hung over him like a storm waiting to break.

His father, Babak, sat beside him, scrolling through the TV, though his attention was divided between the screen and Sebastian. Every now and then, Babak would glance at him, the same proud smile on his face, as if saying, "You've got this."

"First time flying over the Alps, Seb," Babak murmured, leaning in to point out the jagged peaks cutting through the clouds. "How are you feeling?"

Sebastian shrugged, though his stomach was a bundle of knots. "A little nervous, I guess."

Kelly, his mom, sitting across the aisle, gave him a reassuring smile. "It's okay to be nervous, sweetie. It just means you care about doing well. But remember, we're here to have fun too."

Seb nodded, but deep down, he felt the pressure mounting. This wasn't like racing at home in Australia, where he knew the tracks and his competitors. He was heading into the unknown, racing against kids from all over the world—kids who were older, faster, and more experienced. And that thought kept his heart racing.

When they arrived in Italy, the atmosphere was completely different from anything Seb had experienced. As they drove toward South Garda Karting, the sheer magnitude of the event hit him. The track was sprawling, filled with polished team trucks, and bustling with drivers who seemed to know every inch of the circuit. The buzz of excitement and competition crackled in the air, sending a chill down his spine.

Stepping out of the car, Sebastian clutched his helmet, taking a deep breath. His eyes scanned the track, watching as factory teams set up, each with their rows of mechanics and equipment that made Seb's setup at home look modest in comparison.

"We're in a different league now," he thought, biting his lip. But before the nerves could spiral, he felt a hand on his shoulder.

"You okay?" Babak asked, crouching down to meet his son's eyes. There was that steady reassurance again. Seb swallowed hard, nodding.

"Yeah. It's just… big."

"It is," Babak said, his voice calm. "But you belong here, Seb. Look at everything you've accomplished to get here. Just focus on what you do best—drive. The rest will come."

With those words, the weight on Sebastian's chest lightened—just a little. He was here for a reason. This wasn't a fluke. He had worked hard to get to this point, and now it was time to prove that he could keep up with the best.

The Polish Parolin Team welcomed them as soon as they arrived. Stefano, his mechanic, greeted them with a quick handshake and a wide smile, though it was clear that communication would be tricky. Stefano didn't speak much English, and Babak and Seb had to rely on gestures and the few Italian phrases they knew to explain what needed to be done. It was a new experience for Seb—no longer could he rely on his dad to talk him through every step. This time, he had to trust Stefano, trust his kart, and trust himself.

Luckily, Seb had help. Lorenzo Travisanutto, a former KZ2 Vice Champion, was there to coach him. Babak had organised for Lorenzo to be there to guide Seb on his first international race. He had this effortless cool about him, as if he had raced his whole life without breaking a sweat. On their first track walk, Lorenzo pointed out the nuances of South Garda Karting, explaining which corners demanded the most attention and how to handle the sweeping turns with the right amount of throttle.

"See that turn?" Lorenzo said, pointing to a tight hairpin that curved sharply back on itself. "It's all about timing. If you brake too late, you'll lose your line. Hit it just right, and you'll pull ahead."

Sebastian nodded, absorbing every word. It reminded him of the lessons he'd learned back home from Dave, Peter, and Chris, all the mentors who had helped shape him into the racer he was. Their advice rang in his ears: Stay calm. Trust yourself. Don't over-think it.

But it wasn't only Seb who felt the weight of racing in Italy—Babak was grappling with his own sense of awe and doubt. The sheer scale of the competition became apparent as he watched the other drivers surrounded by their teams. Each one seemed to have a full entourage: coaches analyzing every lap, personal trainers ensuring they stayed in peak condition, tutors keeping them on top of schoolwork, and dieticians managing every meal down to the last calorie. Some even had dedicated film crews, capturing every turn, every win, every moment. Babak's chest tightened as he took it all in. *What are we doing here?* he wondered, feeling like they'd wandered into a world so far beyond their reach. *How on earth are we supposed to compete against all of this?*

Standing there, he felt a wave of uncertainty—were they just out of their depth? But then he looked at Seb, who was already preparing for the track, his face set with determination, and Babak knew they couldn't turn back now.

The first few practice sessions were intense. Seb was fast—really fast. Despite being one of the youngest competitors and first time at the track, he found himself keeping up with, and even surpassing, drivers who had been racing internationally for years.

It felt surreal, zipping around the track, knowing that he was on the same stage as some of the best young drivers in the world.

But with every lap, self-doubt still nipped at his heels. "Am I really good enough for this? What if I mess up?"

It wasn't until qualifying that Seb truly began to push those lingering doubts aside. When his lap time placed him on pole in his international debut, a thrill ran through him—a silent validation of all the hours, the sacrifices, and the effort he'd poured into his dream. The weekend was unfolding like a dream.

As the green flag dropped and his first heat began, the roar of engines filled the air, and in that instant, everything else vanished. The doubts, the nerves—they all fell away, replaced by a quiet, unshakeable focus. His eyes locked onto the first corner, his hands steady on the wheel as he nudged the kart into action. He felt the subtle response of the machine beneath him, the way it hugged each curve, responding to his every command.

Through each twist and turn, the world outside the track blurred, and it was only him, the kart, and the road ahead. Each lap sharpened his instincts, his mind zeroed in on every inch of the track. In those moments, nothing else mattered; the weight of the competition, the noise in his head—everything melted away, leaving only the raw, exhilarating drive to race.

Heat after heat, Sebastian kept proving himself. He won several races and even dominated the pre-final, securing pole for his first final in Italy. It was exhilarating, but as he waited on the grid for the final race, nerves crept back in.

"Pole position in the final," he thought, gripping the steering wheel tightly. "This is it."

The race started well. Seb pulled ahead, his kart flying down the straightaways, his heart pounding with every second. But halfway through the race, something felt wrong. The kart wasn't pulling like it had before. The engine felt sluggish, and with every lap, the drivers behind him began to close the gap.

"No, no, no," he muttered under his breath, pushing the kart as hard as he could. But the straight-line speed just wasn't there. One by one, the karts overtook him, and by the time the chequered flag waved, Seb had dropped to 5th.

As Sebastian climbed out of the kart, Babak was already by his side, his expression thoughtful but calm. "The engine gave you a hard time out there," he said, placing a reassuring hand on Seb's shoulder. "But you were fast, Seb. You drove brilliantly."

Seb let out a deep breath, his shoulders slumping. "It was tough, Dad. I just didn't have the power out there to fight properly." He paused, the corners of his mouth lifting into a small, tired smile. "But I'm happy. My goal was to finish in the top ten, and I did better than that."

Babak crouched beside him, wiping some grease off Seb's face with a proud but gentle hand. "Seb, you qualified pole in your first international race, and you still finished in the top five despite everything. That's incredible. Sometimes the race doesn't go your way, but today you proved something much bigger—you belong here, with the best in the world. That's what matters."

Seb nodded slowly, the sting of what could have been still lingering, but Babak's words began to settle in. He glanced back at the track, taking in the grandstands, the other drivers, and the hum of engines in the distance. He was here, in Italy, racing against the best—and holding his own.

When the next weekend rolled around, it was time for the ROK Cup Superfinal—a prestigious international karting event held annually at the South Garda Karting circuit in Lonato, Italy. Organized by Vortex, a prominent kart engine manufacturer, the Superfinal brought together top drivers from various national ROK Cup series worldwide to compete for championship titles across multiple categories. It was a stage like no other, and Sebastian was ready to rise to the occasion. Despite being one of the youngest drivers in the field, he was determined to prove himself against competitors who had raced on this iconic track for years. His performance from the previous weekend gave him confidence, but the engine issues from before still lingered in his mind. What if it happened again?

The weekend started strong—Seb qualified 9th in a field of 89, a solid position given the depth of talent he was up against. With each heat, he clawed his way up the order, winning several and showcasing his grit against seasoned opponents. By the time the final came, he had secured 4th on the grid, an impressive achievement for someone so young in such an experienced field. The nerves were there, but so was his determination, a quiet resolve to show that he belonged among the best.

When the final race began, Sebastian lined up on the grid, his heart pounding with anticipation. Starting from the outside, he knew it was going to be a challenge to hold his position. As the lights went green, the pack surged forward, karts jostling for space on the tight opening corners. Despite his best efforts, Seb got squeezed out, the outside line offering little grip, and he dropped to 8th by the end of the first lap.

"Focus," he told himself, gripping the wheel tighter as he weaved through the chaos. "One position at a time."

Seb's determination kicked in despite the familiar frustration gnawing at him—his engine wasn't delivering the power he needed on the straights. Every time he hit the gas, the kart seemed to lag, losing precious ground to his competitors. Over the next few laps, Seb fought relentlessly, clawing back positions through sheer grit and precision. His overtakes were daring, threading the needle in tight corners where the engine's limitations couldn't hold him back. By mid-race, he had pushed himself up to 5th, but it wasn't easy. Each lap felt like a calculated gamble, relying on his skill in the technical sections to make up for what the engine couldn't deliver on the straights. It was a battle not just with the other drivers, but with the kart itself.

The final laps ticked down, the tension in the air palpable. Sebastian defended his position with everything he had, fending off aggressive challenges from the drivers behind him. It was a test of both his skill and his composure. As he approached the last lap, Seb was still in 5th, his eyes locked on the kart ahead, searching for any opportunity to move up.

Then came the final corner.

Seb braked late, hugging the inside line as he approached the hairpin, determined to hold his position. Just as he prepared to power out of the bend, a sudden impact jarred him—a kart slammed hard into his side, the force reverberating through his body. His kart skidded off the track, the tires screeching against the unforgiving asphalt. He wrestled with the steering wheel, fighting to regain control, but the damage was already done. By the time he re-joined the race, the chequered flag was waving, and he'd slipped to sixth place.

As he pulled into the pits, frustration weighed heavily on him. It wasn't the result he had fought so hard for. But when his eyes flicked to the timing board, a flicker of hope sparked within him—despite the chaos, he'd set the fastest lap during the middle of the heat. It wasn't the victory he wanted, but it was a reminder that he still had the pace to compete with the best.

Back in the pit, Babak was there, as always, waiting for him. "Tough race," he said, pulling Seb into a hug. "But you were amazing out there."

"I wanted to finish higher," Seb admitted, feeling the weight of the day settle in.

"I know. But look at what you've done. You've raced against the best, and you've held your own. You've proven you can do this."

Sebastian glanced around at the other drivers, realizing that Babak was right. He had raced in Italy. He had won heats, secured pole positions, and set the fastest lap of the race. He wasn't just a kid from Australia anymore—he was a competitor on the world stage.

As they packed up to head to their apartment, Seb felt a quiet confidence settling over him. This wasn't the end. It was just the beginning of something much bigger. He had faced the pressure, the setbacks, and the challenges, and he had come out stronger.

And he knew, deep down, that the next time he raced, he'd be ready for whatever came his way.

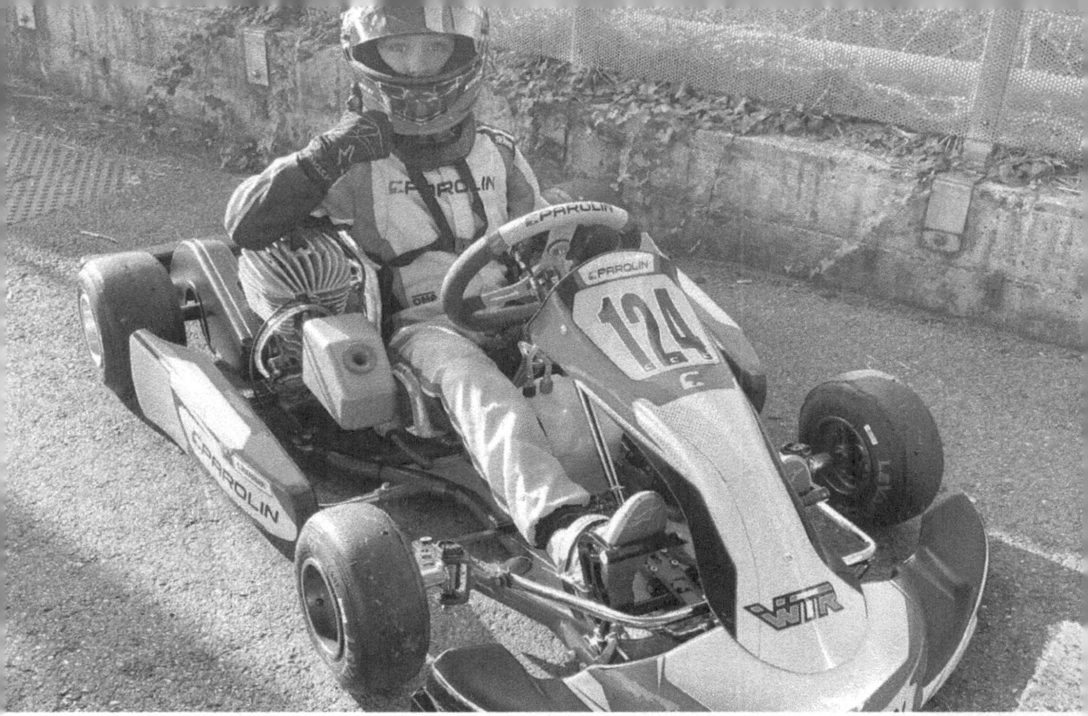

Castrol EDGE
KARTING
SP tools

"GREEN MACHINES AND
NEW BEGINNINGS"

Sebastian sat in the backseat of the rental car, his forehead pressed against the window as the Italian countryside blurred past. He stared at the endless rows of vineyards and vast fields of lush green crops, trying to calm the swirl of thoughts in his head. This was it. He was about to step into a Tony Kart for the first time. The idea felt both thrilling and terrifying.

In front of him, Babak was quiet too, though Sebastian could feel the energy radiating from his dad. He knew what this meant for both of them—a fresh start after everything that had happened with Parolin. Seb had grown used to the familiar red and white of his Parolin kart, the team, and the people he had raced with. But after the frustrations and setbacks in Australia, his dad had made the decision. They were leaving Parolin behind.

"Are you nervous?" Babak finally asked, glancing back at him in the rear-view mirror.

Seb looked up, meeting his dad's eyes. He didn't want to admit it, but the truth sat heavy on his chest. "A little," he said, his voice quieter than he intended.

Babak smiled reassuringly. "It's okay to be nervous, Seb. But you're here for a reason. They see something in you."

Seb nodded, gripping his helmet in his lap. "I just... I hope I do well."

"You will," Babak said, his voice steady. "Just drive like you always do. Focus on the track, on the kart, and everything else will fall into place."

The words helped, a little. But as they pulled into South Garda Karting, the nerves came rushing back. The Tony Kart tent was a sea of green—their iconic colours proudly displayed on the massive rigs and karts. This was a world Sebastian had only dreamed of being part of. He'd watched the Tony Kart team from afar for years, admiring their success, their precision. Some of his ideals, Vettel, Michael Schumacher and Carlos Sainz, all had driven for Tony Kart at one point. Now, he was walking into that world.

Babak parked the car, and they both stepped out, greeted by the unmistakable sound of engines roaring around the track. The air smelled of gasoline and fresh-cut grass, a mix that instantly made Seb feel at home despite the foreign setting.

"Ready?" Babak asked, his voice soft but full of encouragement.

Seb took a deep breath, his fingers tightening around the handle of his helmet bag. "Yeah. Let's do this."

They walked toward the paddock, and soon they were greeted by Alessandro, a friend of Peter Quintiliani, their trusted friend who had helped arrange this test with Tony Kart. Alessandro was all smiles, giving Seb a firm handshake and a reassuring pat on the back. "Ciao, Seb. The Tony Kart mini chassis is a different beast, but you're ready."

Seb smiled, though the butterflies in his stomach fluttered more wildly. He'd never driven a Tony Kart before, let alone with the powerful mini 60 engine. Everything about this felt bigger. He wasn't just here to drive—he was here to prove himself.

They met Lorenzo Camplese, the Italian mechanic assigned to work with Seb. Lorenzo himself was a distinguished driver, with podiums on the world stage. He didn't speak much English either, but the way he moved around the kart, adjusting the setup and giving Seb instructions through a mix of hand gestures and a few broken words, made Seb feel like he was in good hands. There was something about the way Lorenzo and Alessandro worked, meticulous and focused that made Seb trust them immediately.

Seb stood by the kart, watching as Lorenzo tightened a few bolts, his mind racing. He could hear the sound of karts zooming past, feel the vibration in the ground as they sped by. His heart thudded in his chest. He remembered what Chris Schofield , one of his mentors, always told him: "Don't think about everything else. Just focus on your driving. The rest will come."

With a deep breath, Seb pulled on his gloves and helmet, feeling the weight of the moment. This was it—his chance to show what he could do. As he climbed into the kart, the familiar feeling of the seat and steering wheel grounded him. He closed his eyes for a moment, letting the noise of the track fade into the background. This was what he loved. This was where he belonged.

The first few laps were cautious. The kart felt different from anything he'd driven before—lighter, faster, more responsive. It took him a moment to adjust to the power of the mini 60 engine, but with each lap, his confidence grew. The kart flew down the straights, its handling smooth through the corners. Seb began to relax, pushing harder, finding his rhythm.

By the time he pulled into the pit lane, his heart was racing—not from nerves, but from exhilaration. Alessandro greeted him with a grin and a thumbs-up, his satisfaction evident. Babak was there too, his eyes shining with pride.

"How'd it feel?" Babak asked, his voice full of excitement.

Seb pulled off his helmet, his hair damp with sweat, and grinned. "Amazing. It feels so different, but in a good way. I think I could get used to this."

Babak chuckled, patting him on the back. "I think they'll be impressed."

And they were. After the session, Seb sat down with Mr. Robazzi, the head of Tony Kart, and Alessandro, the mini team manager. They talked about his times, his performance, and what they saw in him. There was no rush, no high-pressure sales pitch, just a conversation about potential. And by the end of it, they made an offer—Seb was invited to race with the Tony Kart team in the WSK Final series over the next couple of weeks.

Seb could hardly believe it. As he sat there, nodding along, his heart felt like it was about to burst. Racing with Tony Kart? It was everything he'd dreamed of, and now it was real.

Over the next few days, Seb poured himself into preparations for the upcoming race weekend, fully aware of the challenges ahead. The Tony Kart mini team was small, with just two drivers, and their engines were noticeably underpowered compared to the other teams. The only other driver on the mini team was an Italian boy named Marco, a year older than Seb. They didn't exchange many words—Marco was usually absorbed in his phone, clearly preferring to keep to himself—but Seb didn't mind. He had plenty to focus on: adjusting to the new kart, getting familiar with the team dynamics, and feeling the weight of representing Tony Kart in a whole new league.

The first round of the WSK Final Series was at South Garda Karting. It was a whirlwind. Seb was in the thick of it, racing against some of the best drivers in the world, 123 of them in fact. He was mid-pack for most of the weekend, battling it out with drivers who had been racing these tracks for years. It was tough, they lacked the engine power the other teams had but Seb never gave up. He fought for every position, pushing harder with each heat, out-qualifying and out-racing his Italian teammate.

The races were intense, and though Seb wasn't at the front of the pack, he was always moving up, always improving. Babak and Kelly watched from the sidelines, their hearts in their throats as Seb manoeuvred through the field, overtaking drivers with precision and determination.

By the end of the weekend, Seb had made it into the final and finished solidly mid-pack. It wasn't a win, but it was a start. And for Seb, that was enough. He had proved that he could race with the best, that he could handle the pressure of being part of a prestigious team like Tony Kart.

The final round of the WSK Final Series was at Circuito International Napoli. It was even more challenging. The track was tough—technical, fast, and unforgiving. But Seb was ready. His confidence had grown after the first weekend, and he felt more at home in the Tony Kart.

As the race weekend progressed, Seb continued to push himself, making up positions in every race. He wasn't winning, but he was consistently improving, and that was what mattered. He knew that racing wasn't just about winning—it was about learning, growing, and getting better with each lap.

In the final, Seb started in 19th, fighting his way through the pack with determination, inching closer to a top-15 finish. But on the last corner, disaster struck. Another driver collided with him, pushing Seb off the track. He gripped the wheel tightly, managing to recover, but by the time he crossed the finish line, he had slipped down to 16th place.

As he climbed out of the kart, frustration gnawed at him. He'd worked so hard, clawing his way up from 19th, only to lose out in the final moments. But when Babak came over, pulling him into a hug, the disappointment started to fade. Seb had made it into the top 36 out of 76 drivers, kids who were 2 to 3 years older than him—a huge achievement on such a competitive stage. His teammate hadn't even made the final, but Seb had battled his way through. Maybe 16th wasn't what he'd hoped for, but it was proof he could hold his own among the best.

"You raced your heart out, Seb," Babak said, his voice full of pride. "Sometimes things don't go our way, but you never gave up. That's what matters."

Seb looked up at his dad, the frustration slowly melting away. He had given it everything he had, and in the end, that was enough.

After the race, Mr. Robazzi and Alessandro sat down with Seb and Babak. They had seen enough. Seb had proven himself, not just with his speed, but with his resilience, his determination, and his ability to learn and adapt. They offered him a spot on the team—a chance to return the following year as an official Tony Kart factory driver.

Seb could hardly believe it. At nine years old, he was going to be a Tony Kart driver. It was everything he had worked for, and now, it was happening.

As they left the track that day, Seb looked out at the fading Italian countryside, a sense of pride swelling in his chest.

"A NEW BEGINNING IN ITALY"

At his home track of Ipswich Kart Club, Sebastian sat in his kart, his hands gripping the steering wheel as he waited for the signal to go. The familiar hum of the engine vibrated through his arms, grounding him. He had driven here countless times, the track etched into his memory like the back of his hand. But today, it felt different. Maybe it was because they were only a few weeks away from Italy, from the next chapter of his life, from everything changing. He exhaled deeply and leaned forward, his blue eyes scanning the curves of the track ahead, the place where his journey had begun now serving as a launching pad for his dreams.

"Ready?" Babak's voice called out from the sidelines, where he stood watching with that familiar blend of pride and focus. His dad's arms were crossed, eyes narrowed behind his glasses, but Seb could tell he was tense.

Seb gave a thumbs-up and hit the gas, launching forward. As he weaved through the corners, his mind kept bouncing between the excitement of Italy and the reality that was sinking in. In a few short weeks, he wouldn't be here anymore. This track, his friends, the home they'd lived in for as long as he could remember—all of it was about to change.

"Keep your lines tight, Seb," Babak shouted as Seb passed by again. He was focused, but it was impossible to ignore the excitement bubbling under the surface. Italy. He was going to race for Tony Kart in Italy.

Pulling into the pit lane after his last lap, Seb removed his helmet and shook out his hair, a grin spreading across his face. The kart felt good—really good. The Tony Kart was fast, and every time he got behind the wheel, it felt like it was meant for him.

Babak approached, giving him a nod of approval. "Nice work. You're getting quicker."

"Thanks, Dad," Seb replied, still grinning. "I can't wait to get to Italy. I feel like I'm ready."

Babak smiled, but there was something behind it. It wasn't the usual carefree one Seb was used to seeing. It was tighter, like something was weighing him down. Seb had seen that look more and more lately, especially when his dad didn't know he was watching.

"You will be," Babak said, slapping Seb on the back. "But we've still got work to do. The drivers in Europe are fast—faster than anything you've faced here."

"I know," Seb said. "But I'm ready."

Seb was ready, brimming with excitement for what lay ahead, but what he didn't realize was just how much this move would demand from his family. For Babak, the thrill of Italy and the promise of Seb's racing future were overshadowed by something much heavier—the pressure of holding their lives together financially. They were walking a tightrope, and Seb, lost in the pursuit of his dream, had no idea just how thin the line beneath them had become.

Before they'd left for Italy, Babak's world had started to shift. One day at work, a colleague had pulled him aside, voice serious and unyielding. "You're going to have to decide," he'd said. "The only reason you're able to take your son racing is because you're here with us. But if this keeps up, you won't have a job waiting when you get back." Those words hit Babak like a punch in the gut. He'd always managed to balance family life and work, carefully choosing to keep a job that allowed him the freedom to support Seb's racing without sacrificing their stability. But now, he was facing the cold reality—supporting Seb's growing dreams would cost them far more than time.

The trip had been incredible, but upon their return, the weight of that decision became brutally real. He was called into the office and given the news he'd dreaded. Starting in the New Year, his position would be eliminated. Just like that, Babak had lost nearly 65% of their family's income. The gravity of it settled in his chest, a quiet, constant reminder that this wasn't just a hobby anymore. Every dollar counted, every choice had consequences, and from here on, their lives would be measured against the cost of Seb's pursuit.

Yet, even with the strain and uncertainty, Babak knew where his heart lay. For all the sacrifices, he couldn't deny his son this chance. It wasn't just Seb's dream now—it had become a family's journey, a shared purpose that bound them all together, no matter how steep the road ahead became.

Back home later that evening, Babak sat at the kitchen table with Kelly, his laptop open in front of him. The sound of Seb watching race footage drifted in from the living room, but Babak's focus was on the numbers in front of him. He was running through their finances for what felt like the hundredth time, trying to make it all work.

"You okay?" Kelly asked, noticing the deep furrow in his brow.

Babak let out a long sigh. "I just... I don't know how we're going to pull this off. I've been doing the math over and over, and it doesn't look good. The flights, the housing, the team costs—it's all so much more than I thought. And with losing work..." He trailed off, not wanting to say it out loud.

Kelly leaned in closer, her hand resting gently on his arm. "We'll figure it out. We always do."

Babak shook his head, his gaze distant. "This... this isn't like anything we've handled before," he said quietly, the weight of it evident in his voice. "Seb's poured everything into this dream—every ounce of focus, every free moment, and I don't want him to carry this extra burden. He shouldn't have to think about anything other than that track." He paused, his eyes clouding with worry. "And I can't stand the thought that I might be the reason he doesn't get there."

Kelly's eyes softened. "He doesn't need to know about this right now. Let him focus on racing. We'll handle the rest.'

Babak nodded, knowing she was right, but the knot in his stomach wasn't going anywhere. They were about to leave everything behind for Italy, and the weight of what that meant was growing heavier with every day. He glanced into the living room where Seb was still glued to the screen, analysing every corner and pass from his favourite races. Seb had no idea the sacrifices they were making for him to live his dream. And Babak wanted to keep it that way.

A few weeks later, they touched down in Italy, the excitement of a new adventure buzzing through the air. Seb had his nose pressed to the airplane window, eyes wide as they descended over the rolling hills and red-tiled roofs of the Italian countryside.

"I can't believe we're actually here," Seb said, turning to his parents with a grin. "This is going to be amazing."

Babak smiled, trying to match Seb's energy, but as they drove toward their small apartment, his thoughts drifted back to the numbers. Their new home was modest—just enough for the three of them—but it was a world away from the comfortable life they'd left behind in Australia. Babak felt the weight of each euro spent, each little thing adding to the growing strain he tried so hard to keep hidden from Seb.

When they arrived at Tony Kart headquarters for the first time, Seb's excitement hit another level. The facility was massive, bustling with activity, and filled with karts, mechanics, and drivers from all over the world. Seb was in awe. He couldn't believe he was here, in Italy, about to race for one of the biggest names in karting.

"Ciao, Seb," a voice said, breaking his trance. Alessandro, the mini team manager, smiled as he handed Seb a green-and-white Tony Kart jacket. "Ready to race?"

Seb beamed as he slipped on the jacket, the Tony Kart logo emblazoned across his back. "More than ready."

Babak watched from the sidelines, pride swelling in his chest as Seb took it all in. But alongside the pride was the ever-present worry. This was it—the moment they'd been working toward for years. And yet, the reality of what it had taken to get here, and what it would take to stay, was looming larger than ever.

The racing was everything Seb had hoped for and more. The competition was fierce, the tracks challenging, and the atmosphere electric. But Italy wasn't just about racing. Life in a new country brought its own challenges, too.

Seb's schooling had shifted to home-schooling, which left him feeling a bit isolated from his friends back in Australia. He missed them, and sometimes, the loneliness crept in during quiet moments at home. Kelly, too, was struggling with being so far from her family, from the comfort of the life they'd left behind. And Babak—well, he was managing everything, but just barely.

Each day at the track was a whirlwind. Seb was learning to adjust to the aggressive style of driving in Europe—something he hadn't been used to back home. In Italy, the drivers weren't just fast—they were ruthless. They'd hit you from behind, pushed you off the track, and did not think twice about it.

"DREAMS VERSUS REALITY"

Sebastian sat on the edge of his bed, staring out the window of their small Italian apartment. His Tony Kart jacket hung on the back of the chair, the green and white logo shining brightly in the early morning light. Everything still felt surreal—living in Italy, racing for one of the most prestigious kart teams in the world. At nine years old, he was living his dream. But that excitement came with something else—a knot of nerves that hadn't been there before.

"Seb! Time for breakfast!" his mom, Kelly, called from the kitchen.

Seb stepped out of his room and sat at the table. His dad, Babak, sat there with a cup of coffee, staring into the distance, a frown creasing his forehead. It wasn't unusual—Seb's dad always seemed to have a lot on his mind when it came to racing. But lately, that thoughtful look had grown deeper, like there was something he wasn't saying.

"You ready for another day at the track?" Babak asked, his voice warm, though the smile didn't quite reach his eyes.

"Yeah! I'm ready," Seb said, grabbing a bowl of cereal. "I was watching videos of the Gr3 kids last night. They're so fast!"

Babak chuckled softly. "You're fast too. Don't forget that."

Seb grinned, but a flicker of doubt crept in. Was he fast enough? This wasn't Australia. He wasn't racing kids he'd grown up with. These were the best in the world, and he was starting to wonder if he really belonged here.

As they drove to the track, Seb noticed that his dad wasn't talking as much as usual. He kept glancing out the window, his mind somewhere else. Seb felt like something was wrong, but he didn't ask. He had to stay focused. There was enough to worry about with the racing.

This year, the Mini category had been divided into two groups: the U10s and the Gr3 class, a necessary change due to the overwhelming number of drivers under the age of 13. Among them, Seb stood out as Tony Kart's only representative in the U10 group—a point of pride but also a source of added pressure.

When they arrived at the Tony Kart tent, the atmosphere was already electric. The roar of engines, the rhythmic clinking of wrenches, and the animated voices of mechanics created a symphony of excitement that Seb was growing to love. It was a world of excitement, where every detail seemed to buzz with the promise of racing. Yet, as they walked toward the garage, a flicker of hesitation crossed Seb's face.

Near the line-up of gleaming karts stood Olivier, a sharp-tongued and self-assured 10-year-old North American competing in the Gr3 class for 11- to 12-year-olds. Despite being in the older age bracket, Olivier often practiced alongside Seb and the U10 drivers. From the very beginning, he'd made it abundantly clear—Seb wasn't welcome.

"Hey, Aussie!" Olivier's voice rang out, sharp and taunting. "Try not to get in the way today, all right?"

Seb's stomach twisted. Olivier had been making his life difficult since he arrived. In Australia, everyone was competitive, but it had always felt like family. Here, in Italy, it was different. Olivier was relentless, and worse, he had the older drivers on his side, constantly watching and snickering at Seb.

Seb forced a smile. "We'll see," he said, trying to sound calm. But inside, frustration gnawed at him.

Olivier smirked, his eyes glinting with arrogance. "Why'd they even bring you here? You're just a joke."

Seb clenched his jaw, holding back the words that were bubbling up. He turned toward his kart, focusing on the day ahead. He would prove Olivier wrong. On the track, everything would be different.

Practice started like any other day. Seb slipped into his kart, the familiar vibrations humming through his body as he gripped the wheel. The track at South Garda Karting was one he knew, but it felt different today—more intense, more daunting. His focus narrowed, zoning in on the turns, the straightaways, and the rhythm of the circuit.

But as he approached a tight corner, the sharp thud of a kart hitting his rear jolted him out of focus. His kart skidded, veering off the track and bouncing over the grass. His heart pounded as he wrestled for control, just managing to bring the kart to a stop.

Anger surged through him as he looked around to see who had hit him. Olivier sped by, glancing back to confirm his mark had been left and Seb knew his place.

Seb gritted his teeth. Of course it was Olivier. He had been waiting for a moment like this, to show Seb who was boss. The frustration bubbled up, but Seb took a deep breath. He couldn't let it get to him. Not here, not now.

As the day wore on, the track got busier, and Seb found himself surrounded by the chaos of aggressive driving. In Australia, racing had been about clean lines and precision, but here, it felt like a battlefield. Drivers jostled for position, bumping and shoving as if it were just another part of the race. Seb wasn't used to it, and it showed.

During the second practice session, Seb was trying to get into a rhythm when, out of nowhere, a kart dove inside, cutting him off and forcing him off the racing line. Seb swerved, trying to avoid a collision, but the other driver clipped his side, sending him spinning off the track.

As Seb spun out, he caught a glimpse of the driver—Olivier. As Olivier sped by, Seb didn't need to see his face to imagine the smug look that was undoubtedly there, the one Olivier seemed to reserve just for moments like this. What Seb didn't expect, though, was Olivier turning his head and raising his middle finger in a blatant show of disrespect. The gesture stung, adding insult to an already bitter moment.

Seb's blood boiled. He slammed his fists against the steering wheel, fury clouding his thoughts. He had never experienced anything like this—racing was supposed to be competitive but fair. This wasn't racing; this was war.

When the session ended, Seb climbed out of his kart, his hands trembling with frustration. He didn't know whether to shout or cry. Babak walked over, his eyes scanning Seb's face for an explanation.

"What happened out there?" Babak asked, his voice gentle but concerned.

Seb shook his head, swallowing hard. "It's Olivier. He's messing with me, pushing me around. And... no one cares."

Babak sighed, his expression serious. "I know it's tough. Racing in Europe is different. It's more aggressive, and you're going to have to get used to it. But don't let Olivier get in your head. You're here because you belong here."

Seb wanted to believe him. He wanted to believe that he could handle this, that he was strong enough to push through. But right now, all he felt was frustration.

That night, Seb lay awake, staring at the ceiling of their small apartment. His mind kept replaying the day— Olivier's sneer, the way he had been shoved off the track, the sense of helplessness.

Was this what racing in Europe was really like? Was he cut out for this?

In their small aparment, Babak sat at the kitchen table, papers spread out in front of him. Bills, travel expenses—numbers that didn't seem to add up. Kelly sat beside him, worry etched into her face.

"How are we going to make this work, Babak?" Kelly asked softly, her voice barely above a whisper.

Babak rubbed his face, leaning back in his chair. "I don't know, Kel. I really don't. I've already lost most of my income, and this—this is costing us more than we can afford."

Kelly reached for his hand. "We knew it would be hard. But this is Seb's dream. We can't give up now."

"I know," Babak said, his voice heavy with emotion. "But I'm running out of options. The money's not there. We're barely hold-ing on."

Kelly looked toward Seb's room, her heart aching. "We can't let him know. He's under enough pressure as it is."

Babak nodded, his jaw tight. "He doesn't need to worry about this. Let him focus on racing. We'll figure out the rest."

The next day, Seb returned to the track, his determination hardened. He wasn't going to let Olivier get to him. He had worked too hard, sacrificed too much, to let someone like Olivier take this from him.

But the pressure was mounting. Even though it was only a practice session, Seb could feel the weight of everything pressing down on him—the expectations, the new team, Olivier's taunts, and the aggressive racing. He gripped the steering wheel tighter, his heart pounding in his chest.

As he pulled out onto the track, Seb tried to focus on his lines, driving through the corners, as he worked to find his rhythm. But as he entered a tight corner, Olivier appeared beside him, pushing hard on the inside. Seb braced for impact, and sure enough, Olivier shoved him wide, cutting him off with the same aggressive style he'd shown all week.

Seb's kart skidded, his tires barely holding the track as he fought to regain control. He watched as Olivier sped away, not even glancing back. Anger simmered within him, rising like a tide he struggled to contain, but Seb swallowed it down, determined not to let it get to him. It was just practice, he reminded himself—but still, he couldn't shake the frustration.

He pushed harder, determined to focus on his own driving, knowing he couldn't let Olivier throw him off. Not today. Not ever.

By the end of the session, Seb had finished mid-pack, frustration gnawing at him. As he climbed out of the kart, Olivier walked by, smirking.

"Better luck next time, Aussie," Olivier called out, his voice dripping with arrogance.

Seb clenched his fists, his jaw tight, but before he could say anything, Babak was there, his hand on Seb's shoulder.

"Don't let him get in your head," Babak said quietly. "You've got more talent than he'll ever have. Focus on your race."

Seb nodded, but the sting of Olivier's words lingered.

That afternoon, as they packed up their racing gear, Seb sat on the chair in the team tent, staring at the ground. Babak walked over, his face thoughtful.

"You did good today, Seb," Babak said, sitting down beside him.

Seb shrugged, frustration still simmering beneath the surface. "I don't know, Dad. It's just... hard. I feel like I don't belong here."

Babak looked at him, his voice soft but firm. "You belong here, Seb. It's tough, and it's not always fair. But you're here for a reason. You've got what it takes."

Seb nodded, his dad's words sinking in. He wasn't ready to give up—not yet. There was too much at stake, too much he had worked for.

As they drove back to the apartment, Seb stared out the window at the rolling Italian countryside, determination settling in his chest. This was his dream, and he wasn't going to let anyone—especially Olivier—take it away.

He was ready to fight for it.

"FIRST RACE CHALLENGES –
SOUTH GARDA"

The familiar hum of karts buzzed around him as Seb slide into the seat of his own Tony Kart, and rolled out onto the formation lap. It was his first race in the WSK Super Master Series at South Garda, and everything felt different here. The pressure was heavier, the competition fiercer, and the stakes higher. But Seb had worked for this—every late-night kart prep with his dad, every practice session, every tear of frustration when things didn't go his way. Now, he was about to face it all head-on.

As he warmed his tyres, he clenched his hands around the steering wheel, trying to block out the nerves gnawing at his stomach. He looked up at the grid ahead—he'd qualified 8th. Not bad for his first big race. But it wasn't enough. He wanted more.

From the sidelines, Babak stood watching, his face a mask of calm, though inside, he felt every ounce of pressure that Seb was carrying. He couldn't see his son's knuckles beneath the gloves, but he knew how tightly Seb was gripping the wheel, the tension radiating through his posture. Even with the helmet covering Seb's face, Babak could picture the determined clench of his jaw, the focus etched in his expression. Babak knew the stakes too—he'd sacrificed so much to get here. But today wasn't about the sacrifices; today was about Seb.

"You've got this, Seb," Babak whispered under his breath, as if willing the words to reach him.

Seb's heart pounded, each beat echoing the rhythm of his kart's engine as he rolled slowly around the last corner waiting for the lights to go green in the first heat. Time seemed to stretch, every second thick with anticipation. Then, in an instant, the lights flickered off, and the track came alive with the deafening roar of engines. Seb slammed the gas pedal, feeling the power surge beneath him as he shot forward. Karts surrounded him on all sides, drivers fiercely jostling for position, each vying for every inch of the narrow track. The air was thick with the smell of burning rubber and gasoline, the vibrations of the engine humming through his entire body.

The first few laps passed in a dizzying blur of speed and adrenaline. Seb was locked into a rhythm, his body moving instinctively, reacting to every twist and turn of the track. His hands gripped the wheel tightly, his focus razor-sharp as he navigated each corner with precision, eyes scanning for any opening to slip ahead. Inch by inch, he clawed his way up the pack, determined, relentless. By the end of the heats and pre-final, he'd fought his way up to 5th place overall, a quiet thrill settling in his chest.

For the first time, he felt it—that elusive sense of control, of everything coming together. The kart, the track, the energy around him—it all clicked. It wasn't just about keeping up anymore. He was in the race, fully present, feeling every second as if he were part of the machine itself.

As Seb gridded up for the final, a quiet confidence settled over him. The weekend had been good—his speed, his focus, his rhythm all on point. But this was South Garda, a track as famous for its high speeds as it was unforgiving. Its combination of fast corners and chicane and numerous hairpin's demanded absolute precision. Seb knew that any misstep here could end his race before it even began.

As they rolled off for the formation lap, he took a steadying breath, replaying his race start and strategy over and over in his mind. He pictured each corner, each line, how he'd approach the critical turns. When they rounded the last corner, he was lined up in the third row, his eyes laser-focused on the start lights, waiting for the split-second moment when green would unleash them all.

The lights flashed green, and they were off. Seb surged forward, jostling through the pack to claim a solid position. By the time they reached the first corner, he'd clawed his way to 3rd place—a strong start, exactly where he needed to be. Finding his rhythm quickly, he tackled the track's intense turns with precision, carving through each corner with the confidence of a driver who knew exactly what he was doing.

But as he approached the fast chicane in the middle of the track, a hard, unexpected thud struck him from behind. The impact jolted his kart violently, as if he'd been hit by a freight train. His tires screeched against the asphalt, the entire kart shuddering as he fought to stay upright. In that split second, time slowed down, and Seb felt the helplessness of being thrown off course.

His world spun with the kart, and he could only watch as driver after driver sped past him, disappearing into the distance.

Heart pounding, Seb slammed on the brakes, desperately trying to regain control, but it was too late. In an instant, he'd gone from 3rd place to dead last, left reeling in the chaos of what was supposed to be his shot at victory. The race he had worked so hard for had turned upside down in the blink of an eye.

Seb felt the frustration well up inside, but he kept his grip steady on the steering wheel. He never let his emotions show, especially not now. Instead of shouting or reacting, he took a deep breath, trying to push the disappointment aside. "Why now?" he thought to himself, his heart pounding with a mix of frustration and determination. He could feel the weight of the moment, but he refused to let it define him. This might not have been how he wanted his first race to end, but he wasn't ready to give up. Not yet. "Keep going, Seb," Babak's voice echoed in his mind. "Never give up. Every lap is a chance to come back."

Seb took a deep breath, pushing down the frustration clawing at him. He couldn't let this setback define the race; he still had a shot at salvaging something. After a moment, the kart roared back to life, but the pack was long gone. Determined, he pressed down on the gas, his eyes locking onto the distant karts ahead.

It was a struggle to make up ground. One by one, he began catching up, inching closer to the back of the field. The laps ticked by, and every pass demanded all his focus and strength. He weaved through tight gaps, muscling his way through corners, each move a small victory. Every position he gained was hard-fought, and his body ached from the effort.

In the end, Seb clawed his way up three spots, crossing the finish line in 33rd. It wasn't the finish he'd dreamed of, but he'd refused to give up. As he climbed out of his kart, his body felt heavy, weighed down by exhaustion and the disappointment gnawing at his chest. He took off his helmet, his hair damp with sweat, and stared at the track, still catching his breath.

Babak came over, placing a hand on Seb's shoulder. "You did everything you could out there, Seb. That's all that matters."

Seb looked up, his blue eyes filled with frustration. "I was 3rd, Dad. I could've been up there."

"I know," Babak said quietly, his voice steady. "But you didn't quit. You fought your way back. That's what makes you a champion, Seb—not where you finish, but how you handle the setbacks."

Seb nodded, though the weight of the disappointment still clung to him. It was his first race with Tony Kart, and it hadn't gone how he imagined. But somewhere deep down, he knew his dad was right. He hadn't let the spinout end his race. He'd fought back.

Kelly joined them, her face soft with understanding. "It's just the beginning, Seb," she said, wrapping him in a hug. "You'll have plenty more races. This is just the first step."

As they packed up, Seb replayed the race in his head. Every corner, every move, every mistake. It was a tough start to the season, but he knew racing wasn't just about winning—it was about the journey. And today, the journey had shown him just how hard he'd have to fight.

That night, back at their apartment, Seb lay in bed staring out the window. He thought about the drivers who'd passed him, about how aggressive they'd been. But he also thought about his comeback, how he hadn't let it end there.

As he drifted to sleep, a quiet determination settled over him. There would be more races, more challenges, more setbacks. But no matter what, he would keep fighting. Just like today.

WSK
VORTEX
OMP

551
VORTEX

MG
OMP

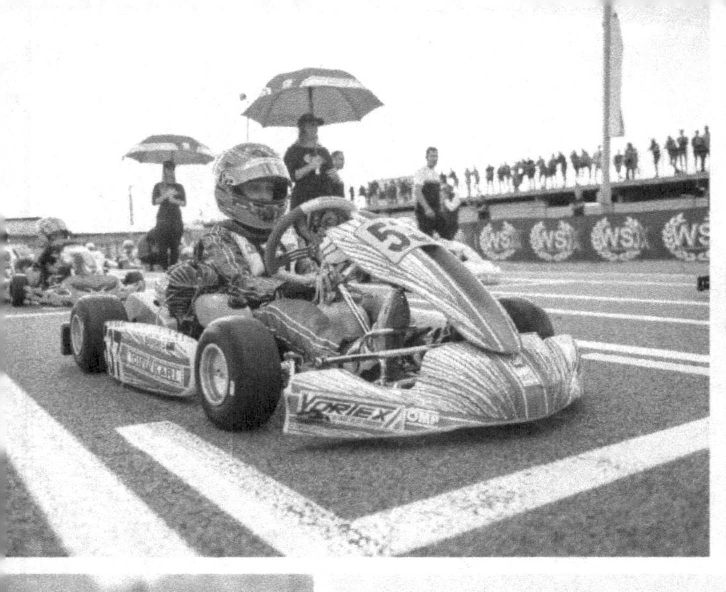

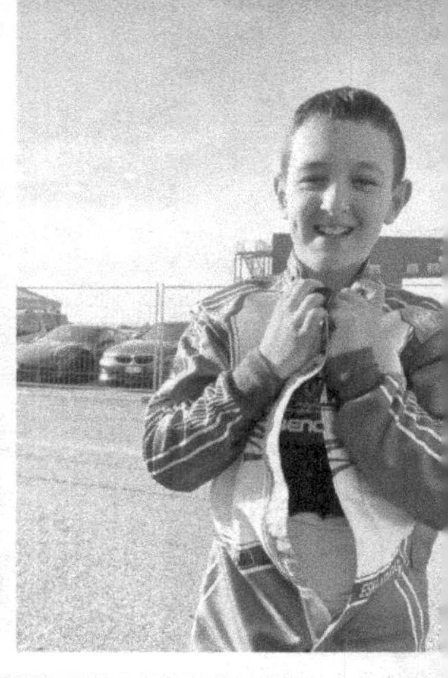

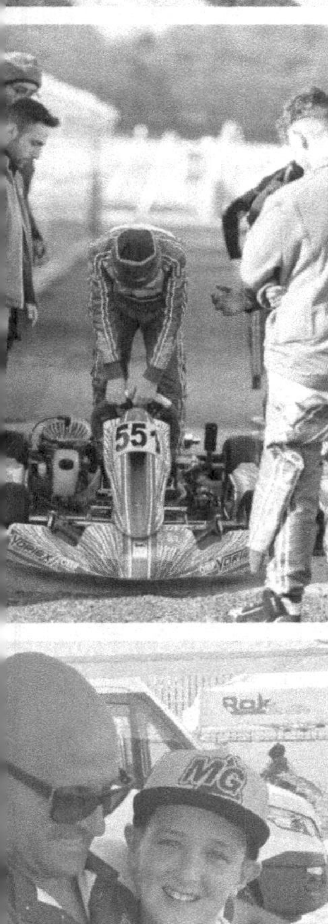

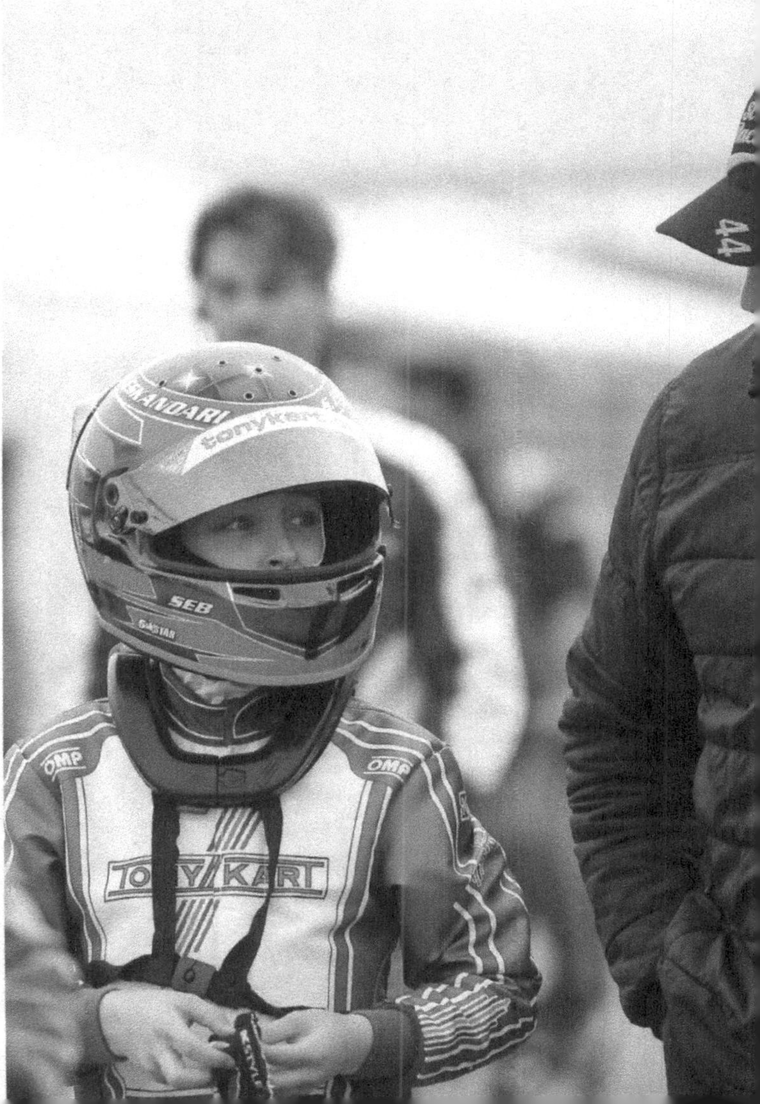
tonykart
SEB
OMP
TONY KART
44

"FRANCIACORTA – A MOMENT OF STRENGTH"

The Franciacorta circuit gleamed under the soft morning light as karts zipped by, their engines roaring. Sebastian stood near his Tony Kart, glancing nervously at the other drivers who had gathered in the pits. It was the second round of the WSK Super Master Series, and the pressure was mounting. He wasn't just racing to win—he was racing to prove that he belonged.

Seb adjusted his gloves, pulling them tighter over his small hands. His nine-year-old frame felt almost swallowed by the race suit, but his heart pounded fiercely in his chest. The older kids stood nearby, chatting and laughing, but their words weren't friendly.

"Think you're ready for this, little guy?" Olivier, sneered as he walked past Seb. Olivier was almost 11, two years older than Seb but noticeably shorter. Despite his smaller size, Olivier carried himself with a smug confidence that made Seb's stomach twist.

"You sure you don't want to sit this one out?" Olivier added, his voice dripping with mockery.

Seb tried to ignore the jabs, focusing on the track ahead, but the teasing only continued. The other drivers joined in, feeding off Olivier's taunts. Every word felt like a punch to Seb's gut. His throat tightened, and despite his best efforts to stay calm, he felt his eyes burn with unshed tears.

Don't cry. Don't let them see you cry, he repeated to himself, taking a shaky breath. But the pressure was too much. Everything—the distance from home, the weight of his dreams, it all crashed down on him. And now, this. He turned away quickly, wiping his eyes.

Babak, his father, noticed the tension in his son's posture. From the sidelines, he had been watching Seb closely, sensing that something wasn't right. He walked over, his expression calm but concerned.

"Seb," Babak said gently, crouching beside him. "What's going on?"

Seb bit his lip, trying to hold it together. "It's nothing, Dad. Just—just the other guys." He glanced over at Olivier and the others, who were still whispering and chuckling.

Babak followed his gaze, his jaw tightening ever so slightly. He didn't need to ask to know what was happening. He put a hand on Seb's shoulder, grounding him. "Listen, Seb. You're here because you earned it. You've worked hard, harder than anyone else. Don't let them get inside your head."

Seb nodded, though the weight in his chest still felt heavy. "I know, but it's tough, Dad. They keep pushing, and I'm just... tired."

Babak's eyes softened. "I get it. But you've always been strong. You don't need to prove anything to them. Just go out there and drive for yourself. That's all that matters."

Seb took another deep breath, feeling the knot in his stomach loosen a little. His dad was right—he didn't have to prove anything to anyone but himself. Racing wasn't about showing off or pleasing others. It was about doing what he loved. He could feel the resolve building within him again.

The announcement for qualifying crackled over the loudspeakers. Seb slid his helmet on, pulling the visor down, his eyes still glassy from the tears. Babak gave him a reassuring pat on the back. "Go get 'em, Seb."

As Seb drove onto the track for qualifying, the roar of the engine drowned out his thoughts. This was where he felt most at peace—in the kart, with nothing but the hum of the motor and the curves of the track to focus on. The teasing faded into the background, replaced by the sharp focus that only racing gave him.

He gripped the wheel, his body moving instinctively with each turn. His kart hugged the corners, his foot pressing just enough on the throttle. Lap after lap, he pushed harder, feeling the adrenaline surge through him.

When the final times came in, Seb had done it. Pole position.

He pulled into the pits, his heart racing. Babak was there, beaming with pride. "I told you," Babak said with a wide grin. "You've got this."

But Seb's moment of triumph didn't last long. The heats that followed were brutal. Racing in Italy wasn't like the clean, respectful driving Seb was used to back in Australia. Here, it was a battlefield. Drivers bumped into each other deliberately, karts jostling for position with little regard for the rules.

In his first heat, Seb started well. He kept the lead at the start and was leading going into the fast double right hander on the first lap when he felt the familiar thud of a kart hitting his from behind. His kart jerked to the left, the rear wheels losing grip as he skidded wide. The other drivers flew past him as Seb struggled to regain control. By the time he got his momentum back, he was down 4 spots.

Heat after heat, the same thing happened. Whether it was a kart nudging him wide on a corner or forcing him onto the grass, Seb couldn't catch a break. It was frustrating, but he refused to give up.

By the time the final race came around, Seb was starting from 16th position. His body ached from the constant strain, and his mind felt clouded with the chaos of the heats. But he hadn't come all this way to let a few bad races knock him down.

As the lights went out, Seb surged forward, determined to claw his way up. Staring on the outside row resulted in him losing five positions, dropping him down to 21st. He stayed focused and pushed through the pack, navigating the tight turns and long straights with precision. The aggressive tactics of the other drivers still caught him off guard at times, but Seb had learned to adapt.

With each lap, he found his rhythm, weaving through the chaos. The teasing, the rough driving—it all faded away as he focused solely on the race. In the end, Seb crossed the finish line in 9th, a far cry from the pole position he had started with, but it felt like a victory in its own right.

As he pulled into the pits, Babak was waiting for him. There was no need for words. Seb could see the pride in his father's eyes, even though he hadn't won.

"You did it, Seb," Babak said, his voice steady. "You fought back."

Seb took off his helmet, his chest heaving from the effort. "It was tough out there, Dad," he said, his voice trailing off as he tried to make sense of the mix of emotions swirling inside him.

Babak smiled softly. "You showed them what you're made of, Seb. That's what matters. You didn't let them get to you."

Seb looked down at the kart, the paint still scraped from the hits he'd taken during the heats. He nodded, feeling the weight of his dad's words sink in. This race had been about more than just winning—it had been about standing tall, even when the odds were stacked against him.

Later that night, back at their small apartment in Italy, Seb sat on his bed, scrolling through pictures of the day's race on his dad's phone. His body still ached, and the frustration of the heats lingered in his mind. But something had shifted. He knew this journey wasn't going to be easy. It was going to test him in ways he hadn't expected.

But as long as he had his family, as long as he had the drive to keep going, he knew he could handle it.

Seb glanced over at Babak, who was sitting at the kitchen table, looking over bills and paperwork. A pang of guilt hit him, knowing how much his parents were sacrificing for him to race. He hadn't understood the full weight of it before, but now, seeing the exhaustion on his dad's face, he could see it clearly.

"Thanks, Dad," Seb said quietly.

Babak looked up, surprised. "For what?"

"For everything," Seb said, his voice steady. "For believing in me."

Babak's expression softened, and he nodded. "Always, Seb. Always."

And as Seb lay down that night, the ache in his body a reminder of the day's struggles, he knew that this was just the beginning. There would be more challenges ahead, more tough races, but he was ready. With his family by his side and his heart set on the future, he could face whatever came next.

"FIRST PODIUM AT SOUTH GARDA – A BREAKTHROUGH"

Sebastian stared out at the South Garda track, the hum of engines filling the air. It was a familiar sound now, one that used to make his heart race with nerves. Today, it made his chest tighten for a different reason. The pressure was still there, but something else lingered—hope. He was back at South Garda for the WSK Open Series, a track where he'd faced so many challenges before. But this time, it felt different. Maybe it was the air, or maybe it was the way the sun cut through the morning fog, but Seb had a feeling that today, something might finally click.

"Hey, you ready?" Babak asked, his voice steady, though Seb could sense the hint of tension behind it.

Seb turned to his dad and nodded, adjusting his gloves. "Yeah, I'm ready."

Babak ruffled his son's hair, the gesture both comforting and familiar. "You've worked hard for this, Seb. Just remember, focus on the race, not the result."

Seb bit his lip, nodding again, but he couldn't help it—he *wanted* the result. For weeks, he'd been clawing his way through the races, fighting for every position, but a podium finish had always seemed just out of reach. He was determined that this time, things would be different.

The day started off better than he expected. He qualified 10th, which wasn't pole, but it was solid, giving him a chance to fight his way forward in the heats. As the heats progressed, Seb found himself getting into a rhythm. The kart felt smooth under him, the track almost welcoming him back. He fought hard, weaving through the field with each lap, and by the end of the heats, he had clawed his way up to 2nd place for the final grid.

Seb sat in his kart on the starting grid, taking a deep breath as he looked around. The other drivers were just as focused, their eyes set on the challenge ahead. His heart raced, but he pushed the nerves down. This wasn't new anymore. He belonged here.

As the lights went out, the karts roared to life, and Seb pushed forward, gripping the wheel tightly as he aimed for the first corner. But the pack was aggressive, and despite his best efforts, he lost a few positions in the chaos. He gritted his teeth, frustrated, but he didn't let the setback consume him.

"Focus. Stay calm. There's still time."

The words echoed in his mind, a reminder of the lessons his dad had drilled into him over the years. Racing wasn't just about speed; it was about patience, strategy, and resilience. Seb knew that all too well. And today, he would prove it.

Lap after lap, he fought his way back, making daring overtakes and holding his line through the tight corners. The roar of the crowd blurred into the background as he locked into the rhythm of the race. By the time the final laps rolled around, Seb had worked his way back to 3rd. His heart pounded in his chest, adrenaline rushing through his veins as he pushed harder, his eyes fixed on the karts ahead.

But as much as he pushed, the top two drivers had a lead he couldn't quite close. Still, 3rd was his. He could feel it. As the chequered flag waved, Seb crossed the line, his body buzzing with exhaustion and exhilaration.

He'd done it.

Seb pulled into the pits, his breath coming in short bursts as he climbed out of the kart. He felt the weight of the moment settle on his shoulders—a mix of disbelief and pride.

Babak was the first to reach him, pulling him into a tight hug. "You did it, Seb! First podium in WSK. I'm so proud of you!"

Seb smiled, leaning into his dad's embrace, feeling the warmth of the moment sink in. "I—I can't believe it."

"You should. You earned this," Babak said, pulling back to look at him. There was pride in his eyes, but also something else—something Seb couldn't quite place.

"Are you okay, Dad?" Seb asked, noticing the way Babak's smile didn't quite reach his eyes.

Babak hesitated for a moment, glancing away before sighing. "I am, Seb. It's just... I'm heading back to Australia soon."

Seb's heart sank. He'd known this was coming—his dad had work back home—but now, hearing the words, the reality hit harder than he expected.

"For how long?" Seb asked, his voice quieter now.

"A few months, at least. You and Mom will keep racing, and I'll join you as soon as I can."

Seb nodded, trying to swallow the lump in his throat. He'd never raced without his dad by his side. It had always been the two of them. And now, with his first real breakthrough, the thought of doing it without him felt daunting. But he couldn't let that show. He had to be strong—for himself and for his dad.

"I'll be okay," Seb said, trying to sound confident. "You've taught me enough. I'll just keep racing."

Babak smiled, but Seb could see the emotion in his eyes. "I know you will. You're stronger than you realize, Seb."

The podium ceremony was a blur. As Seb stood there, holding the trophy in his hands, the weight of it felt different than he'd imagined. It was heavy, not just because of the metal, but because of everything it represented—months of hard work, sacrifices, and now, the bittersweet moment of success mingled with the knowledge that his dad would be leaving soon.

Kelly was there, too, her eyes shining with pride as she hugged him tight after the ceremony. "I'm so proud of you, Seb. You've worked so hard for this."

"Thanks, Mom," Seb whispered, the words feeling too small for everything he wanted to say.

As the evening sun dipped behind the mountains, casting a golden glow over the track, Seb sat, the trophy resting beside him in the backseat. He had finally made it to the podium. The rush of adrenaline and joy had begun to fade, replaced by the quiet realization that it wasn't the end of the journey—it was only the beginning.

Seb stared out the window as they drove away from the track, his heart heavy, knowing that the day's victory was bittersweet. Babak would be leaving tonight, heading back to Australia for work, and Seb wasn't sure how he'd face the next few months without him.

Kelly glanced at Seb in the rear-view mirror, her eyes soft but worried. "You okay, sweetie?" she asked gently, knowing how much this transition was weighing on him.

Seb nodded, though the lump in his throat made it hard to speak. "Yeah," he mumbled, gripping the trophy a little tighter. It felt like a fragile promise he was afraid might slip through his fingers if he let go.

The car ride to the airport was quiet, the hum of the engine the only sound as the city lights blurred past. Babak, seated in the front, glanced back at Seb, a small smile on his face, but his eyes were filled with the same uncertainty Seb felt. None of them knew how things would be once Babak was gone, but they were all pretending like it was okay.

When they pulled up to the airport terminal, the air seemed heavier than before. Seb's stomach churned as they got out of the car, and he followed his dad toward the entrance. Babak's suitcase rolled behind him, the wheels making a soft clicking sound on the pavement, each click feeling like a countdown to when he would leave.

Babak turned and knelt down in front of Seb, placing his hands on his son's shoulders. "You did great today," he said, his voice steady. "I'm so proud of you."

Seb nodded, blinking back the sudden sting of tears. He didn't want to cry, not here, not in front of his dad. He needed to be strong, like Babak always was.

"I'll be back before you know it," Babak continued, his voice softer now, as if he could sense Seb's struggle to keep it together. "And until then, you keep pushing. You've got this, Seb."

Seb swallowed hard and nodded again. "I know, Dad."

Babak pulled him into a hug, holding him tight. For a moment, Seb allowed himself to lean into the embrace, to feel the comfort of his dad's presence before it slipped away.

Kelly stood beside them, her face a mix of pride and sadness. She hugged Babak next, whispering something Seb couldn't hear, and then it was time. The goodbye that none of them wanted had arrived.

As Babak walked toward the security line, Seb stood beside his mom, watching as his dad turned back one last time to wave. Seb waved back, his hand heavy, and watched until Babak disappeared into the crowd of travellers.

On the drive back to the apartment, Seb stared out the window, the city lights now feeling colder and distant. His chest felt tight, but he forced himself to take a deep breath, just like his dad had taught him. He could handle this. He had to.

When they arrived back at the apartment, Seb went straight to bed, but sleep didn't come easily. The adrenaline from the race still buzzed in his veins, and every time he closed his eyes, his mind replayed the final laps, the podium, and then the moment his dad disappeared into the airport. It all felt so overwhelming.

How was he going to race without his dad there?

Seb rolled onto his back, staring at the dark ceiling, listening to the faint hum of the fan. His mind raced with a million thoughts, but eventually, one rose above the rest—his dad believed in him. Babak wouldn't have left if he didn't think Seb could handle it.

Racing isn't just about speed, his dad's voice echoed in his mind. *It's about heart. And you've got more of that than anyone I know.*

Seb took a deep breath and closed his eyes, letting the tension in his body slowly melt away. He could do this. His dad was right. He'd worked too hard to let fear or doubt stop him now.

The next morning, Seb woke up with a quiet determination. The weight of the previous night still hung in the air, but it wasn't as heavy as before. He dressed quickly, already thinking about the next race, the next challenge. He knew his dad would be proud of him for pushing forward.

Seb and Kelly left the apartment, walking down the stairs, the world felt different—quieter, lonelier—but the track was still out there waiting for him. And so was the work. He couldn't slow down now.

Kelly placed a hand on his shoulder. "Ready to go, champ?"

Seb nodded, forcing a small smile. "Yeah. Let's get back to work."

As they left, Seb's heart still ached a little, but he held onto the feeling of the podium beneath his feet, the trophy in his hands, and the knowledge that no matter what happened next, he was moving forward.

There was still work to do.

"LIFE IN ITALY – STRUGGLES FOR THE FAMILY"

The streets of Lonato were quieter than Seb was used to. Even though it was Italy, and life seemed to hum with a certain energy, everything felt different now. It had been a few days since Babak had returned to Australia for work, and their small apartment felt emptier with each day that passed. The faint sounds of scooters zipping by and the distant chatter from cafés did little to fill the space his dad had left behind.

Seb sat at the kitchen table, staring at his laptop, a math lesson open on the screen, but his focus was miles away. His mind wandered back to the track, to the feel of the kart beneath him, the sound of engines roaring, the thrill he missed more than anything. Home-schooling was lonely, a far cry from the familiar buzz of a classroom and the laughter of friends. But sacrifices had to be made. Racing meant leaving things behind.

Kelly moved around the kitchen, preparing breakfast, but she was quieter than usual. Seb noticed the heaviness in her movements, like she was carrying an invisible weight that had only grown since Babak left. She'd glance up and smile if she caught his eye, but even then, he could see past it.

"You okay, Mom?" Seb asked, breaking the silence.

Kelly paused, one hand on the coffee pot, and for a moment, Seb thought she'd brush it off, and reassure him. Instead, she sighed, the kind that held back more than it let out, and finally smiled at him, softer this time. "I'm okay, sweetie. Just... thinking about things. About life, you know?"

Seb nodded, not pushing her. He knew what she meant. Moving to Italy hadn't just changed his life; it had transformed theirs. They'd traded their routine back in Australia for an unpredictable life in a foreign country, one that revolved around racing, home-school, and the gaps left by Babak's absence.

"Do you miss home?" he asked quietly, keeping his eyes on the laptop screen, as if the answer might be easier if he didn't look at her.

Kelly walked over and sat down beside him. "Of course I do," she said, resting her hand over his. "I miss my family, your dad, and our friends. But we're here because of something bigger, Seb. You're chasing your dream, and that makes all of this worth it."

Seb felt a familiar tightness in his chest, a weight he usually kept hidden. She was here because of him, because of the racing, because of a dream they all carried. He hated the pressure of that sometimes, the silent burden of knowing how much his family was giving up.

"It's hard, though," he muttered, running a hand through his hair. "Sometimes I feel like I'm missing out on so much. My friends, school... It's just different here."

Kelly squeezed his hand. "I know, Seb. But you're not alone. I'm here, and we'll figure this out together."

Grateful for her words, Seb nodded, but deep down, he couldn't shake the loneliness. Home-schooling isolated him from the world he once knew. His only classmates were pixels on a screen, no schoolyard, no lunch breaks with friends. Every day was just him, his laptop, and Kelly.

The days at the track were different, of course. There, he felt alive. But even then, the teasing from some of the older kids made it hard. They didn't know what it was like to leave everything behind for a dream. They didn't know how much was riding on each race, how every success felt like a small victory for not just him, but for his family.

"Do you think Dad's okay?" Seb asked suddenly.

Kelly hesitated, her eyes flicking to the window where the sunlight streamed in, casting soft shadows on the floor. "I think he's doing what he has to do," she said finally. "It's hard for him too, being away from us. But you know your dad—he believes in you, Seb. He wouldn't have left if he didn't think you could handle it."

Seb nodded, but the familiar ache of missing his dad settled in his chest. It wasn't just about the races. Babak had always been his rock, his steady presence at every practice, every race. Now, it was just him and Kelly, trying to navigate this new life.

Later that afternoon, they headed to the track for practice. Seb felt more at home there, but even the track felt different without his dad. He got into his gear, slipping on his gloves and helmet, trying to push the homesickness away.

As he revved the engine, the vibrations travelled up through the steering wheel, and for a moment, everything else faded. This was where he felt in control. Out here, it didn't matter if he was home-schooled, if he missed his friends, if his dad was on the other side of the world. Out here, it was just him and the kart, the track laid out in front of him like a puzzle waiting to be solved.

But the isolation followed him, even on the track. There were moments when he'd glance over at the pit lane and half-expect to see his dad standing there, nodding in approval or giving him a thumbs-up. Instead, it was just Kelly, her face a mixture of pride and concern, trying to fill the gap Babak had left.

After practice, Seb felt the weight of it all pressing down on him. He sat in the kart, his helmet still on, staring out at the emptying track. He loved racing, but he hadn't expected this part—the loneliness, the feeling of being torn between two worlds. His friends back home probably didn't even know what it felt like to sit in a kart at a world-class track, but Seb didn't know what it was like to sit with them at lunch, to joke about weekend plans or school crushes.

"Seb?" Kelly's voice broke through his thoughts. "You ready to pack up?"

Seb nodded, pulling off his helmet and running a hand through his sweaty hair. "Yeah. Let's go."

As they loaded his gear bag into the car, Kelly looked over at him. "You're quiet today," she said gently.

Seb shrugged, not wanting to burden her with his thoughts. He knew she was struggling too. "Just thinking."

"About what?"

He hesitated, then finally said, "Everything, I guess. I miss Dad. I miss home. I miss... how things used to be."

Kelly nodded, her face softening. "I know, sweetheart. I miss it too. But we're here now, and we've got to make the best of it. Your dad is working hard so you can have this opportunity, and I know it's tough, but you're not alone."

Seb bit his lip, the weight of her words settling over him. He wanted to make the most of it. He wanted to be the racer his family had sacrificed so much for him to become. But sometimes, it felt like too much.

"I'll try," he said quietly, though the words felt small.

Kelly smiled and pulled him into a quick hug. "That's all I ask."

As they drove home, Seb sat there, looking out the small window, his mind racing with thoughts of the track, of home, of all the people who believed in him. A soft breeze drifted through, carrying the faint scent of the countryside, grounding him. He didn't have all the answers, and he didn't know what tomorrow would bring, but his mom's words echoed in his mind: *You're not alone.* With a deep breath, he nodded to himself. Whatever it took, he'd keep pushing. For his dad, for his mom, and for himself.

"THROUGH TRIALS, WE RISE"

The road stretched out before them as Seb and Kelly left behind the familiar surroundings of Lonato. Days of emotional and physical exhaustion weighed heavily, but the move felt like a step forward. Their new destination was a small, renovated barn nestled on a sprawling farm between the Cremona and Casteletto tracks. From the outside, it looked like something out of a postcard—a rustic, picturesque retreat surrounded by endless fields under the Italian sun. For a brief moment, Seb felt a flicker of excitement. This place seemed different, like a quiet escape from the relentless pace of their racing life.

But as soon as they stepped inside, the charm began to fade. A strong, sulfuric smell filled the air, lingering like a stubborn shadow in the room. Even the water from the tap carried that sharp, unmistakable scent, as if the sulfur had seeped into the very walls. Kelly did her best to mask it, filling the barn with air fresheners and lighting candles in every corner, but sometimes, especially at night when the air was still, the smell felt overwhelming. A wave of nausea would rise, making it impossible for her to feel settled. She kept reminding herself that this was temporary, just another chapter in their journey. But as she lay in bed each night, eyes closed, breathing through the discomfort, she couldn't shake the feeling of the weight they were carrying—each sacrifice piling on top of the last.

One night, after Seb had gone to bed, Kelly sat at the small kitchen table, attempting to lose herself in a book. The quiet barn creaked around her, the sulfuric smell a faint but constant reminder of their surroundings. Suddenly, a slight movement caught her eye, making her freeze. A scorpion, its tail curved and ready, was creeping across the floor. Her heart pounded as she quietly reached for her sandal, gripping it tightly before bringing it down with all her strength. Even after the scorpion was gone, her skin prickled with unease, a reminder of just how far they were from the comforts of home. From that night on, she checked everything twice, never leaving shoes on the floor and inspecting every corner with caution.

Hoping for a break from the relentless challenges, they planned a small getaway for the Easter weekend, deciding to drive to a nearby town with a pool to unwind. But ten minutes into the drive, the dashboard warning light blinked on, and Seb immediately noticed.

"Mom, what's that light?" he asked, a frown creasing his forehead as he stared at the dash.

Kelly let out a sigh, steering toward a small gas station up ahead. "It's the tire pressure warning. I'll check it out when we stop."

When they pulled over, Kelly spotted the problem right away—a large screw was lodged in the sidewall of the tire. She opened the trunk, hoping to find a spare tire, but all she found was a repair kit, completely useless for a punctured sidewall. She managed to inflate the tire just enough to get them to a nearby auto shop.

The mechanic quickly assessed the situation, but unfortunately, he didn't have the right tire in stock. After making a few calls, he found another shop twenty minutes away and convinced them to stay open a little longer for them. By the time they arrived, both Kelly and Seb were weary, the day's plan of relaxation having slipped away. But the kindness of the shop staff, who worked swiftly and showed genuine interest in Seb's racing journey, brought a small comfort to them both. Seb beamed when they asked questions about his affiliation with Tony Kart, feeling a sense of pride that eased some of the day's frustration.

When they finally returned to the barn late that evening, Seb felt lighter, grateful for the unexpected kindness they'd encountered. But the barn's smell greeted them as soon as they opened the door, a reminder of the challenges they were still up against.

The next morning, just as they were settling back into a routine, another problem arose. Strange gurgling noises began echoing from the bathroom. Kelly pressed her ear against the wall, listening intently before flushing the toilet to see if it would settle. Instead, the water started rising alarmingly fast, threatening to spill over the rim.

"Seb!" she called out, panic tightening her voice. "Call Dad! Ask him what we should do!"

Seb fumbled for his phone, dialling Babak. As he explained the situation, Babak listened calmly, suppressing a chuckle at the situation. "Try using the toilet brush like a plunger," he suggested.

With a mixture of desperation and determination, Kelly followed his advice, managing to fix the immediate issue. But the incident left both her and Seb drained, each minor inconvenience adding to the weight they were already carrying.

Despite these everyday struggles, Seb and Kelly had a bigger goal in mind. They knew that if they were going to stay in Italy long-term, they'd need proper visas, and for that, a more permanent residence was essential. Their days off became filled with apartment viewings, often met with wary glances from landlords and real estate agents hesitant to rent to foreigners.

"Another rejection?" Seb asked one afternoon, his voice tinged with disappointment.

Kelly forced a reassuring smile, though her own frustration was growing. "It's hard to convince them, Seb. But we'll keep trying. We'll find somewhere."

After weeks of searching and countless rejections, they finally met Elena, a kind real estate agent who seemed genuinely interested in helping them. She listened patiently to their story and promised to speak with her boss on their behalf. By the end of the week, she called them with good news—an apartment had just opened up, and they were welcome to lease it.

The apartment wasn't perfect. It was on the fourth floor of an old building, accessible only by a winding, narrow staircase. But to Seb and Kelly, it was everything. They finally had a home base, a place where they could settle, somewhere that didn't smell of sulfur or come with scorpions lurking in the shadows.

That night, as Seb lay in his new room, surrounded by the familiar comfort of his things, a quiet sense of calm washed over him. For the first time in weeks, he felt like he could truly breathe. The struggles, the homesickness, the countless sacrifices—they all felt worth it in this moment. Here, he could focus, could train, could pour himself into racing without the constant disruptions.

Yet, as he closed his eyes, a familiar ache surfaced—the ache of missing his dad. Babak was still thousands of miles away, a steady, comforting presence that felt achingly distant. Seb clutched his phone, staring at the screen, tempted to call just to hear his dad's voice. But he knew Babak would tell him to rest, to focus on the race ahead. So he let himself feel the ache, the weight of everything they'd been through, and the hope that someday, all these sacrifices would be worth it.

"VICTORY AT LA CONCA – FIRST WSK CHAMPIONSHIP"

Sebastian stood at the edge of the La Conca circuit, the early morning sun casting a golden glow over the track. The crisp air carried the scent of gasoline and rubber, and the sound of engines warming up buzzed in the background. This world—Italy, karting, and the endless pursuit of speed—was his now. But today felt different. Today, something bigger lingered in the air.

Returning to Italy had been anything but straightforward. Just days earlier, Seb and Kelly had wrapped up a whirlwind trip back home, a journey driven by the need to finalize their visas. But the homecoming had been a bittersweet one; the rush to secure all the paperwork meant they barely had time to catch their breath. The minute they landed, they were thrust into a world of bureaucratic red tape—a maze of forms, signatures, and endless queues that felt like they'd never escape.

They spent the first day shuttling between the Poste and the Questura, each location insisting they needed a stamp or a signature from the other. The lines were long, the waiting rooms cold and crowded. It was a game of administrative ping-pong, and by midday, Seb could see the wear on Kelly's face, her frustration peeking through despite her best efforts to stay calm.

"Didn't they say this was the last stop?" Seb asked, glancing up at his mom as they stood outside yet another office, holding a handful of forms they'd been told to re-fill.

Kelly sighed, attempting a reassuring smile as she brushed a strand of hair out of her face. "Apparently not. We just need to keep pushing through," she said, her voice gentle but carrying the exhaustion of the day.

In that moment, Seb felt a wave of guilt, realizing the weight his mom was carrying for him to be here, to chase a dream that was both theirs and his. He didn't say it, but a silent promise formed in his mind: *I'll make this worth it, Mom. I won't let you down.*

Hours later, they were directed to a building that seemed more like a fortress than a government office, tall iron gates and stone walls looming before them. It was intimidating, and if not for a group of people clustered at the entrance, Seb might have thought they had the wrong place. Fortunately, a passer-by—a migrant worker who overheard Kelly asking for help—gestured for them to follow him inside, understanding the frustrations of the system all too well. He spoke to the receptionist in rapid Italian, navigating the procedures and helping Kelly submit the last few documents.

With everything finally completed, they left the office with a sense of exhausted relief. "Maybe now," Kelly murmured as they walked back to their car, "we can catch our breath."

Seb looked over, seeing the weariness in her eyes. It hit him how much his mom was giving up, how every moment of frustration and exhaustion was a sacrifice for him. And he knew he had to make it all worthwhile.

Now, standing on the track at La Conca, those frustrations seemed miles away. Seb's mind wandered to when he'd first watched the WSK races on YouTube, marvelling at the speed and skill of the drivers, the pride on their faces when they stood on the podium. Ian Salvestrin's voice had made each pass and corner feel monumental. "Someday, that'll be me," Seb had told himself back then.

After his race weekends, Seb would sit down to watch the recordings, catching his breath each time he heard Ian mention his name. "Sebastian Eskandari on the move"—it was surreal. He'd crossed into a world he once only dreamed of, with Ian's familiar voice narrating his moves, making it all feel real. He wasn't just a kid back in Australia watching from his room anymore; he was living it.

Between heats, Ian often found Seb in the paddock, always offering encouraging words. Seb hung onto those words as they reminded him of why he'd started racing, of the dream that had kept him going even on the toughest days. "This weekend might be his weekend," Seb thought, letting himself believe it for a moment.

The past few months had been tough—filled with gruelling races, long nights of reflection, and countless moments where he had to push through doubt. But today, at the WSK Super Cup, he felt something he hadn't felt in a while: pure, quiet confidence. He took a deep breath, his fingers tracing the worn edges of his gloves as he prepared.

From the sidelines, Kelly watched him, her hands wrapped around a cup of coffee, her gaze following his every move. She was his constant, the quiet support he needed when everything else felt overwhelming. And Babak? Though he wasn't there in person, Seb felt his dad's encouragement echoing in his mind.

"Hey, ready?" Kelly asked, her voice soft but full of encouragement.

Seb nodded, pulling down his visor. "Yeah, I am." He whispered the words almost like a promise, more to himself than anyone else. He slid into the kart, feeling the familiar jolt of adrenaline. He was starting the final race on pole after qualifying fifth and climbing through the heats. With each race, his confidence had grown, and now, here he was, the final race about to begin.

Seb glanced to his left, catching sight of a familiar figure in the bright white kart beside him. His grip tightened instinctively. This boy wasn't just any competitor—he was fast, reckless, the kind of driver who'd push the limits to claim a spot, no matter the cost. Time and again, he'd forced Seb off track, costing him podiums that had felt so close. Seb's jaw set as he remembered each hard-earned position lost in the last laps to this boy's aggressive moves.

He took a steadying breath, feeling the tension coiled within him. The marshal raised the flag, and Seb's fingers tightened further on the wheel as they rolled off on their formation lap. Today, he'd race smarter, stronger.

When the lights went out, everything happened in a blur. Seb surged forward, but he caught something out of the corner of his eye. The driver next to him had jumped the start, edging forward before the lights changed. Seb could've reacted, but he remembered what he'd learned: racing wasn't just about being fast; it was about racing smart.

He settled behind the leader, staying close, knowing the penalty would come soon enough. Focusing on his line, Seb hit each corner with precision, conserving his energy for the final laps. He didn't need to take unnecessary risks. For now, his strategy was patience.

The penalty board lit up two laps in. The leader had been given a penalty, and Seb felt a surge of adrenaline but kept his focus. Seven laps. He could do this.

The roar of the engine filled his ears, every move calculated, his heart steady as he kept pace. By the final lap, Seb was still in second, but he knew he didn't need to overtake. All he had to do was finish strong. He crossed the line in second place, but a flood of pride washed over him. He knew what that penalty meant. He'd done it.

Seb slowed down, pulling into the pits, and saw the penalty board still flashing. The reality hit him—he'd won. He pulled off his helmet, feeling the cool air and the weight of his victory all at once. This was it. His first WSK Championship.

Kelly was there in an instant, pulling him into a hug. "You did it, Seb! You really did it!"

Seb nodded, the emotions overwhelming. The track, the karts, the people around him—all faded into the background. For this moment, it was just him and his mom, sharing the victory they had worked so hard for.

"I knew you could do it," Kelly whispered, her voice thick with emotion. "You've worked so hard for this."

Seb pulled back, a smile spreading across his face. "I couldn't have done it without you, Mom. Without Dad. Without all of it."

As Seb stood on the podium, lifting the trophy high above his head, he felt its weight, heavier than he'd imagined, yet solid and reassuring in his hands. This wasn't just a trophy; it was a symbol to everything he'd overcome, every sacrifice his family had made to help him reach this moment. His heart swelled as he looked up, seeing the Australian flag displayed proudly in the number 1 position, his national anthem filling the air. He glanced over at Ian, who stood at the sidelines with a thumbs-up, pride written all over his face. Seb's smile grew wider; this victory wasn't just his. It belonged to everyone who had believed in him, everyone who had shared in the dream.

That night, back at their apartment in Poggiardo, Seb sat quietly, the trophy resting beside him on the table. Kelly was on the phone with Babak, filling him in on every detail. Seb didn't need to hear the words to know how proud his dad was. Instead, he stared at the trophy, thinking about tomorrow, about the next race, about everything he still wanted to achieve.

He lay down that night, feeling the exhaustion of the day settling over him but unable to shake the excitement bubbling inside. Today had been monumental, but tomorrow? Tomorrow held even more. He was no longer just chasing a dream—he was living it. And as he drifted off to sleep, the weight of that realization settled in, feeling like a promise.

He had won his first WSK Championship, but what he had gained was so much more. With hard work, patience, and the right mindset, Seb knew there was nothing he couldn't accomplish. The road ahead was long, but he was ready. Every twist, every turn, every challenge—he was ready.

panta
RACING FUEL
VEGA
MGtires
Racing
WSK
WORLD
WSK SUPER CUP by Mi
eo Nazionale Gr.3 ACI Ka
WORLD CIR   LA CONCA (I
7 - 1   2023
MGtires
Racing
VEGA
panta
LIBE

nale MINI Gr.   by Mini
WORLD CIR   T LA   Karting
7 - 1   E 2   A (I)
MGtire
Racing
WSK
VEGA
panta
RACING FUEL
LIBE
TIT
WSK
LORANDI
baby
racing tia

"CHALLENGES AND GROWTH"

The warm glow of victory from La Conca still lingered in Sebastian's mind. His first WSK Championship win was everything he'd dreamed of, a moment that proved he could race with the best. But as the second half of the year rolled in, the challenges became sharper, the victories more elusive.

But it wasn't just racing that had been on his mind. Italy was a world away from Australia, yet in many ways, it felt familiar. Seb quickly discovered that some things remained the same no matter where you were—like the thrill of racing and the friendships that came with it. Although he missed his friends back home, Seb embraced the adventure. He began to pick up Italian phrases, surprising himself by how quickly he could understand people around him. He even made friends in the paddock—Maximus, Niccolo, and Bruno—other racers who shared his passion. Between heats, they'd joke around, sharing stories and laughing at each other's accents. Bruno and Niccolo taught Seb all the best

Italian hand gestures, and Maximus was a gentle friend with mutual respect, someone that Seb had a lot in common with and they just understood each other. Together, they helped him feel like he belonged, no matter how far he was from home.

But now it was time to focus. Seb adjusted his gloves and slipped on his helmet, the world narrowing to the kart and the track before him. The roar of engines surrounded him as he prepared for the next race. He'd been so close in the last few rounds, but something always seemed to go wrong—a dropped chain here, an engine failure there. And then, of course, there were the other drivers, always willing to bump him off track if it meant gaining an inch.

The familiar pit of determination sat heavy in Seb's stomach as he waited for the signal to start. It wasn't that he hadn't expected challenges—he knew racing was never easy—but the series of setbacks tested him in ways he hadn't anticipated. Every time he strapped into the kart, he could feel the weight of expectations—his own, his family's, the team's. And then there was Babak, thousands of miles away in Australia, missing from the track but never far from Seb's thoughts.

"Focus, Seb," he reminded himself, tightening his grip on the steering wheel. The red lights blinked off, and the race began with the usual chaos of engines roaring and karts jostling for position.

Seb darted through the pack, weaving around the other drivers, his kart responding to his every move. For a few brief moments, it felt like everything was under control. The rhythm of the race, the hum of the engine, it all clicked into place. But as he neared the end of the straight, disaster struck.

A hard bump from behind sent his kart lurching to the side. Seb clenched his teeth, fighting to keep control, but it was too late. The impact had knocked him off balance, and he spun out, his kart skidding across the asphalt. He watched helplessly as kart after kart zoomed past him.

By the time Seb righted himself and got back into the race, he was at the back of the pack, a cloud of frustration hanging over him. But there was no time to dwell. He pushed forward, overtaking one kart, then another, the adrenaline pushing him to claw his way back through the ranks.

When the chequered flag waved, Seb had managed to finish in the middle of the pack. Not great, but not a complete loss either. Still, it stung. He pulled into the pits, his heart pounding, his body heavy with exhaustion and frustration.

Kelly was waiting for him, her face a mix of pride and concern. "You did great, Seb," she said softly, brushing a stray hair from his sweaty forehead as he pulled off his helmet. "I saw what happened out there."

Seb nodded, biting back the sting of disappointment. "It's just... frustrating, you know? I was doing everything right, but then someone hits me, and it's like all that hard work goes out the window."

Kelly gave him a sympathetic smile. "I know, sweetie. But you always bounce back. And you're still learning, still getting stronger with every race. That's what matters."

Her words, as always, carried a quiet reassurance, but Seb couldn't help the knot that tightened in his chest. He missed having Babak there, missed his dad's calm advice and steady presence. And though Kelly was doing everything she could, the void left by Babak's absence was hard to ignore.

Later that night, Seb lay in bed, staring up at the ceiling. His body ached from the day's race, but it wasn't the physical pain that weighed on him. It was the constant pressure to be better, to prove himself again and again, even when things went wrong.

His phone buzzed on the nightstand, and Seb grabbed it, seeing a message from Babak.

Babak: "Tough race today, but I'm proud of you. You're learning more from these challenges than you would from easy wins. Keep your head up, Seb. I believe in you."

Seb sighed, reading the message twice before setting the phone back down. He knew his dad was right, but sometimes, it felt like the setbacks were piling up too fast. But what choice did he have? He had to keep going, had to push through.

The next race weekend brought more of the same. Seb qualified well, making it into the top five, but once again, things fell apart during the final. An engine failure cut his race short, leaving him stranded on the sidelines as he watched the other drivers cross the finish line.

He'd barely made it out of his kart when he felt the heat of frustration rising up in him. It wasn't fair. He was doing everything right, but the mechanical failures, the bumps and crashes—it all seemed like too much.

Kelly wrapped her arms around him in a quick hug. "It's not your fault, Seb. Sometimes, things just don't go your way."

"I know," Seb muttered, trying to keep his voice steady. "But it feels like no matter how hard I try, something always gets in the way."

Kelly squeezed his shoulder. "And that's what makes you stronger. Every time something goes wrong, you learn. You're becoming a better driver with every race, even when it doesn't feel like it."

Seb wanted to believe her, but the weight of it all was getting heavier. It wasn't just about winning anymore. It was about proving to himself—and to everyone else—that he deserved to be there.

Despite the setbacks, Seb remained consistent in his performance. Even when things went wrong, he still managed to finish in the top three in several races. And as the season wore on, something began to shift.

The Tony Kart team, which had started with only a few drivers, began to grow. New faces joined the team, eager and competitive, but Seb held his own. His consistency, even in the face of bad luck, had earned him respect.

It was during one of the last races of the season that Seb truly felt the difference. His kart was running smoothly, and though he wasn't leading, he was right up there with the top drivers. For the first time in weeks, everything felt like it was clicking into place.

As he crossed the finish line in third, a wave of pride washed over him. It wasn't the win he'd hoped for, but it was a hard-fought podium. And for the first time in a while, he felt like he was making real progress.

Kelly met him at the pits, her face beaming. "You did it, Seb! Another podium!"

Seb smiled, feeling the weight of the race lift off his shoulders. "Yeah... I did."

But even as they celebrated, Seb knew that the road ahead would only get tougher. The challenges weren't over. But he was ready for them. He'd grown stronger with each setback, and now, he was ready for whatever came next.

As they packed up to leave, Seb glanced back at the track, feeling a mix of pride and determination. This season had tested him in ways he hadn't expected, but he was still standing, still racing.

And that was something no one could take away from him.

"STEPPING UP – THE FINAL RACE AT SARNO"

Sebastian stood outside the Tony Kart garage, clutching the gleaming La Conca trophy in his hands. The air was crisp, filled with the familiar hum of mechanics tuning engines and drivers preparing for the final round of the WSK Euro Series. But Seb wasn't thinking about the race just yet. Instead, he was staring down at the trophy, the one he'd earned just weeks before. His first WSK Championship win—it had been monumental, but he knew he hadn't done it alone.

Taking a deep breath, he walked inside the garage, where Alessandro, the team manager, was bent over a kart, speaking to a mechanic in rapid Italian. Seb hesitated for a moment, his fingers brushing against the cool metal of the trophy.

"Alessandro?" Seb called out, his voice wavering slightly.

Alessandro straightened up and turned around, wiping his hands on a rag. "Sebastian, what's up?" His thick Italian accent made the words sound smooth, even comforting.

Seb swallowed, then held out the trophy. "I want you to have this."

Alessandro blinked, confused. "What? Why?"

Seb shifted on his feet, his heart thudding in his chest. "Because it wasn't just my win," he said quietly. "It was a team effort. You believed in me. I wouldn't have been able to do it without you and the team. So... I want you to put it up at the factory, next to the other trophies."

Alessandro's face softened, and for a moment, Seb thought he saw a flicker of emotion in the usually stoic man's eyes. "Grazie, Seb," Alessandro said, taking the trophy with a gentle smile. "That means a lot. We'll put it somewhere special."

As Seb walked out of the garage, he felt lighter, as if a weight had lifted off his shoulders. He didn't need the trophy as a reminder of the win. The victory was inside him, in the confidence he'd built over the season. Now, his focus was entirely on this weekend—on Sarno.

This weekend was different. Seb was moving up to the Gr3 class, racing against older, more experienced drivers. The nerves had been building in his stomach since the moment they arrived, but as he glanced at the track, the familiar determination settled over him. He was ready.

The weekend started off strong. Seb qualified 5th, placing himself right at the front of the pack for the heats. It was a solid performance, especially for his first time in Gr3, and though the competition was fiercer, Seb was determined to prove he belonged.

Saturday night, back at the hotel, Seb lay in bed, staring at the ceiling. His mind replayed the laps from the day over and over, analysing each corner, each overtake. He felt the pressure more than ever, especially now that he was competing in a higher class. But despite the nerves, there was excitement, too. This was what he had been working for—the chance to race with the best.

His phone buzzed beside him, and he picked it up to see a message from Babak.

Babak: "Saw your quali result! 5th in Gr3, that's awesome, Seb. You've got this."

A smile tugged at Seb's lips as he typed out a reply.

Seb: "Thanks, Dad. I'll do my best."

Babak's encouragement had always been his rock, even from afar. Seb missed him being at the track, but knowing his dad was watching from home made it a little easier. They were still in this together, even if they were miles apart.

The final day arrived, and Seb felt a mix of excitement and tension bubbling inside him. He'd raced well in the heats, starting the final in 6th. It wasn't pole, but it was a good position—one where he could make moves.

As he climbed into his kart, the familiar roar of the engines surrounded him, the air thick with the smell of gasoline and the buzz of anticipation. Seb pulled on his gloves, tightened his helmet strap, and took a deep breath. This was it.

The lights blinked off, and the karts shot forward. Seb immediately darted into position, navigating the first few corners with precision. He could feel the intensity of the race, the other drivers fighting for every inch of track. But Seb was holding his own, climbing quickly and taking the lead after turn 2.

It was a great start. He sped down the back straight hitting 118km/hr. And then, out of nowhere, his teammate attempted a late move into the hairpin, hitting Seb, forcing him wide. Seb's heart dropped as he saw the other karts zoom past. His team mate's move had cost them both positions, and now Seb was scrambling to recover.

Frustration surged through him, but he swallowed it down, focusing on the race. There was no time to be angry. He had to keep pushing, had to claw his way back.

But something had shifted. Seb's rhythm was off, his focus shaken. He fought hard, overtaking where he could, but it wasn't enough. By the time the chequered flag waved, Seb had slipped all the way down to 26th.

As he pulled into the pits, Seb felt a crushing sense of disappointment. He climbed out of the kart, pulling off his helmet, the sting of what could have been weighing heavy on his chest.

Kelly was there, waiting for him. She wrapped him in a hug, her voice soft and soothing. "You did your best, Seb. It's just one race."

Seb nodded, though the frustration lingered. "I know. I just... I had it. And then..."

"Sometimes things don't go the way we plan," Kelly said gently. "But you've shown everyone that you belong in this class. You're racing with the best, and you're holding your own."

Seb looked at her, his heart still heavy, but her words slowly began to sink in. She was right. This was just one race, one weekend. And even though it hadn't gone the way he'd hoped, he was still growing, still learning.

Later that evening, as the sun dipped below the horizon and cast a warm glow over the emptying track, Seb stood alone, watching the Tony Kart crew methodically pack up. Shadows stretched across the asphalt, but his mind was focused inward, sifting through the memories of the season—moments of triumph, grit, and the relentless tests that had pushed him further than he ever imagined. This race might have been a setback, but it was only a small chapter in a much larger story.

Standing there, he felt an undeniable sense of belonging. The Tony Kart mini team wasn't just a team—they were family. Alessandro, the team manager, was like a second father, guiding him with unwavering support and wisdom that reminded him of his own dad. Then there was Lorenzo, his mechanic from earlier in the year, who treated him like a little brother, sharing tricks of the trade and laughing with him over small victories. Gabriel, the quiet, focused data and tech specialist, watched over him like an older sibling, pushing him to analyze each turn, each mistake, to always improve.

Seb felt a swell of gratitude rise within him. With these people and his mum by his side, his dad rooting for him from across the world, and his own resolve burning stronger than ever, he knew he could face whatever challenges lay ahead.

Babak's words echoed in his mind, reminding him of all the lessons he'd learned over the years: *Racing isn't just about winning. It's about heart. It's about pushing through when things don't go your way.*

As Seb looked out at the track, he realized something. This weekend wasn't a failure—it was a stepping stone. He had faced a challenge, and while he hadn't come out on top, he had kept going. He had kept racing. And that, more than anything, was a victory.

The next morning, as they prepared to head back to the apartment, Seb spotted Alessandro near the team truck, the La Conca trophy still gleaming on the shelf inside.

Seb walked over, his heart lighter now. "I'll get another one," he said, his voice steady.

Alessandro smiled, clapping him on the shoulder. "I have no doubt, Seb. No doubt at all."

And with that, Seb turned and headed toward the car, already thinking about the next race. Because while the road ahead was long, he knew one thing for sure—he was ready for whatever came next.

"TOUGH DECISIONS – SEB'S STRUGGLES"

Seb sat on the edge of his bed, staring out the window at the faint glow of the early morning sun creeping over the horizon. His racing suit was draped across the back of a chair, and his helmet sat on the floor next to his worn-out shoes. Normally, the sight of his gear would fill him with excitement. But today, it brought a wave of uncertainty.

His body had changed so much over the past few months. He had grown taller, his arms and legs now slightly too long for the sleek kart he'd driven all season. The kart didn't handle the same way it used to. It was like fighting the machine to keep control, especially around tight corners. It had become... unpredictable.

Seb sighed, running a hand through his hair. He had always been able to trust the kart, to feel the track beneath him, to know instinctively when to push and when to hold back. But now? Now, every time he went into a corner, he held his breath, hoping the kart wouldn't flip.

Seb was now racing in the WSK Final Series. Babak had come back to Italy for the last two races. After watching from afar all year Babak was possibly more excited than Seb to see him on track again.

Practice and the heat races had tested Seb more than ever this weekend. The previous day's crash at the hairpin of Mechanics Corner replayed vividly in his mind, each detail etched into his memory. He could still feel the heavy jolt of the impact—how another kart had rammed into his side, sending a shudder through his entire body as his kart spun out of control. He remembered the helpless feeling as he tried to regain control, only to be thrown hard into the wall. The sound of screeching tires, the scraping of metal against asphalt, and the sharp pain that shot through him all came flooding back every time he thought about it.

Physically, he'd walked away unscathed, but the mental toll lingered, settling like a weight in his chest.

The knock on the door startled him out of his thoughts.

"Seb?" His dad's voice was soft, but there was concern laced through it. "You okay, buddy?"

Seb turned toward the door, finding Babak standing in the doorway, his expression as worried as Seb felt.

"I don't know," Seb admitted, his voice barely above a whisper.

Babak stepped into the room, sitting down on the edge of the bed next to him. He didn't say anything for a moment, just looked at his son, waiting for him to continue.

Seb took a deep breath, feeling the weight of his decision pressing down on him. "I don't think I can race," he finally said, the words heavy on his tongue. "The kart... it doesn't feel right. I'm too tall now, and it flips when I go into corners. And the crash..."

Babak's brow furrowed, and he nodded slowly. "It's been tough lately," he said quietly, placing a hand on Seb's shoulder. "But we can figure this out. You don't have to race if it's not safe. Your safety comes first, always."

"I know," Seb replied, biting his lip. "But it feels like I'm giving up if I don't race. What if everyone thinks I'm just... scared?"

Babak's grip on his shoulder tightened, his eyes filled with re-assurance. "Choosing not to race because it's unsafe isn't giving up, Seb. It's smart. It's mature. You're not afraid of racing—you're just listening to what your body and your instincts are telling you. That's the sign of a true driver. Knowing when to push, and when to step back."

Seb nodded, but the frustration still gnawed at him. This wasn't how he wanted to end the season. He had worked so hard, and now it felt like his own body was betraying him.

"I just wish I could finish strong," he said softly, staring down at his hands.

"You've already had an incredible season," Babak reminded him. "You've shown everyone what you're capable of. One race isn't going to change that."

Later that morning, Seb sat in the Tony Kart garage, watching the other drivers prepare for the final day of racing. The mechanics buzzed around, fine-tuning the karts, the sounds of tools and engines filling the air. Normally, he would be in the thick of it—putting on his gloves, getting ready to go. But today, he sat on the sidelines, feeling like an outsider in the place that had been his home for so long.

It was the right decision. He knew that. But that didn't make it any easier.

He stood up, walking over to where Alessandro, the team manager, was speaking with a group of mechanics. When Alessandro saw Seb approach, he paused, giving him a sympathetic look.

"Sebastian," Alessandro said, his voice gentle. "How are you feeling?"

Seb took a deep breath. "I've decided not to race," he said, the words coming out stronger than he expected. "It's just... it's too dangerous with how the kart's handling right now. I don't want to put myself or anyone else at risk."

Alessandro nodded, his expression understanding. "I respect that, Seb. It's a tough call, but it's the right one."

Seb swallowed the lump in his throat. "Thanks, Alessandro."

After a brief moment of silence, Seb glanced around the garage. He knew this was goodbye, at least for now. The season was over, and so was his time with Tony Kart. It was bittersweet—he had so many good memories here, but the last few weeks had been hard, and it was time to move on.

Before he left, Seb made his way around the garage, saying goodbye to the mechanics, the hospitality staff, and even the chefs who had always made sure he had his favourite pasta after a long day of racing. Each farewell was accompanied by words of encouragement, and it was clear that despite the struggles, Seb had earned the respect of the team.

When he finally walked out of the garage with Babak and Kelly by his side, there was a quiet sense of closure. The sun was setting, casting a warm golden glow over the track, and for the first time in a while, Seb felt... at peace.

As they packed the car, ready to head back to their temporary apartment in Italy, Babak's phone buzzed. He glanced at it, his eyebrows raising in surprise.

"What is it?" Kelly asked, curious.

Babak's lips twitched into a smile. "It's a message from another team manager. They're interested in Seb."

Seb's eyes widened. "What? Already?"

Babak chuckled, holding up his phone. "Looks like word travels fast. They want to know if you'd be interested in testing with them."

Seb blinked, the weight of the past few days momentarily lifting. "Really?"

Babak nodded. "Really."

Kelly placed a hand on Seb's shoulder, squeezing gently. "See? This isn't the end. It's just another beginning."

As they climbed into the car, Seb stared out the window, watching the Italian countryside blur past. He still felt the sting of disappointment, but there was something else now, too—a flicker of hope.

His journey wasn't over. Far from it. This was just one chapter ending, and somewhere ahead, a new one was waiting to begin.

For the first time in days, Seb allowed himself to smile.

There were new opportunities on the horizon, and he knew that no matter what challenges came his way, he had the strength to face them.

Because he wasn't just a driver. He was a racer.

And racers never stop moving forward.

"TESTING THE WATERS"

Sebastian's heart raced as the familiar outline of South Garda Karting came into view, the morning sun casting long shadows across the legendary track. It felt like home in some ways—he had raced here many times before, he knew the bends and straights—but today was different. Today, he was testing in the OKN-J class, with Ward Racing, a step into a faster, more competitive world. It was a leap forward, one that brought excitement and nerves in equal measure.

He glanced out the window of the car as they pulled into the paddock. His mom, Kelly, sat in front of him, quietly sipping her coffee, and Babak, his dad, drove, glancing at Seb in the rear-view mirror.

"Ready to go buddy?" Babak asked, his voice calm but with that familiar undertone of pride and encouragement.

Seb nodded, though his stomach felt like it was full of butterflies. "Yeah, I think so. It's just... different. Faster."

"You've been ready for this for a long time," Babak reassured him. "It's just another step."

Seb took a deep breath. His dad always knew how to make things sound simple. But Seb knew this was a big day. Testing with Ward Racing, a Swedish team known for its speed and competitiveness, wasn't just about learning to drive a faster kart. It was about proving that he could handle the step up, that he could push himself to a new level.

As they pulled to a stop, Ben George, who had helped organize the test, waved from across the paddock, walking over to greet them.

"Morning, champ!" Ben called out, his usual smile wide. "How are you feeling?"

Seb climbed out of the car, adjusting his jacket against the crisp Italian air. He felt a rush of nerves but also excitement. "Excited," Seb admitted, glancing toward the track. "But, you know, a little nervous too. The speeds are faster than what I'm used to. OKN-J is no joke."

Ben nodded thoughtfully, clapping a hand on Seb's shoulder. "That's normal. Everyone feels that way when they step up to something new. The key is not to try and conquer it all at once. Start slow, build your pace. By the time you're halfway through, you'll feel like you've been racing in this class forever."

Seb smiled a little at that, feeling the knot in his stomach loosen just a bit. Ben's confidence in him always helped steady his nerves. "Yeah, I'll take it easy at first."

"Good man," Ben said, nodding toward the track. "You'll be fine. Trust me, you'll surprise yourself."

Seb walked toward the pit area where the team had already prepped the kart. The sight of it—a gleaming green Tony Kart chassis with the Ward Racing logo—made his pulse quicken. The kart was beautiful, a mix of sleek power and potential. And yet, the thought of climbing into it and hitting speeds faster than he'd ever experienced in a kart made his fingers tingle with anticipation.

Babak and Kelly watched him as he suited up, their presence grounding him. His mom gave him a small wave, mouthing "Good luck," and his dad simply nodded, as if saying, "You've got this." They believed in him, and that was everything.

Sebastian pulled on his gloves and helmet, the familiar weight of them settling over him like armour. The helmet's visor clicked into place, and suddenly, the world outside dimmed. It was just him and the track now.

Seb climbed into the kart, sliding into the seat, his hands gripping the steering wheel through his thick gloves. Unlike the mini karts he was used to, the OKN-J required more than just pressing a button to start—it was all about timing and coordination. He felt the weight of the kart beneath him, more powerful, more intense. His mechanic, standing behind, signalled him with a nod. Seb took a deep breath, placing his foot lightly on the throttle, waiting for just the right moment.

Ben leaned in, giving a thumbs-up. "Remember, easy does it. Get a feel for it."

"Ready?" the mechanic called, bracing himself behind the kart.

Seb nodded, his heart racing. The mechanic gave the kart a hard push, and Seb pressed the throttle, pulling the compression switch at exactly the right moment. The engine roared to life beneath him, the vibrations shaking through the frame like a living, breathing thing. It was a wild animal, and now, it was in his hands.

He slowly rolled onto the track, the familiar hum of rubber on asphalt filling his ears.

The first lap was cautious. Every muscle in his body was alert, every corner approached with care as he felt out the limits of the kart. The power was immense, and he could feel the difference in every acceleration, every turn. The speed built up gradually, lap by lap, as Seb's confidence grew. His hands, once tense on the wheel, started to relax, and soon, the kart responded to him in a way that felt almost instinctual.

By the fourth lap, something shifted. The kart wasn't just fast—it felt like an extension of him. Each corner came smoother, each straight felt endless as the engine roared, propelling him forward. The nerves that had weighed him down at the start were gone, replaced by the quiet thrill of focus and control.

He could feel himself pushing, edging closer to the kart's limits with each lap. He knew the track well, but the speed was new, and he embraced it.

Halfway through the day, Seb noticed something strange—he was as fast as the OKJ times. The drivers who were supposed to be faster, more experienced, were clocking slower laps than him. A flicker of disbelief washed over him. Was this really happening? Was he actually faster than the more experienced class?

He pushed a little harder, shaving milliseconds off his time with each lap. The kart responded perfectly, like it was made for him. The feeling was electric, a rush of adrenaline that surged through his veins as the lap times dropped.

When the day finally ended, Seb pulled into the pits, his heart still racing. He had completed 7 sessions and almost 100 laps. As he removed his helmet, he caught Ben's wide grin. Babak was already walking over, pride glowing in his eyes.

"How'd that feel?" Ben asked, his tone suggesting he already knew the answer.

Seb couldn't help but smile, his pulse still hammering. "It felt… amazing. I didn't think I'd get that fast."

"You didn't just get fast," Ben said, shaking his head. "You were faster than the OKJ drivers out there today. That's no small feat."

Seb blinked, the weight of that statement sinking in. He had been pushing hard, but faster than OKJ? That was supposed to be a class 0.5 seconds quicker per lap. A sense of pride mixed with disbelief settled over him. He had exceeded even his own expectations.

As they stood there in the pit lane, the team owner, Joakim, walked over, his face serious but impressed. "Sebastian," he said, his accent thick but his tone warm, "you've done very well today. I think you're ready for more."

Seb looked up, his heart swelling with pride. To hear that from someone like Joakim—an established name in karting—was huge.

"Thank you," Seb said, his voice steady though his mind was racing.

"Keep this up, and I think we'll see a lot of success," Joakim added with a nod, before turning to speak with his team.

Seb watched him go, still processing everything. It was hard to believe that just a few hours ago, he had been nervous about stepping into a faster class, and now here he was, impressing everyone—including himself.

As he packed up for the day, Seb couldn't help but reflect on how far he had come. The challenges of the season, the setbacks, the triumphs—it all felt like part of a larger journey, one that was just beginning. Today wasn't just about speed or lap times. It was about proving to himself that he could step up when it mattered, that he belonged in this faster, more competitive world.

As they drove away from the track, Seb leaned back in his seat, a sense of calm washing over him. This wasn't just another practice day—this was a turning point. He wasn't simply a kid in a kart anymore; he was becoming a driver, stepping into a world that felt like it had been waiting for him. In the junior kart, everything felt right—like it finally fit him. After the recent frustrations of feeling confined by the limitations of the mini kart, where his size had become more of a hindrance than an advantage, this was a fresh start. For the first time in what felt like ages, he wasn't battling against the machine but he felt truly connected to it. It wasn't just a new chapter; it was the beginning of a journey toward something far greater, something that now felt firmly within his grasp.

But even with all that success, he couldn't forget Ben's words: "Take it slow, build your confidence." Because as thrilling as today had been, Seb knew that this was only the beginning. There was so much more ahead, so many more challenges to face.

And he was ready for them.

"GOING HOME, GOING JUNIOR"

Sebastian stared out the window as the plane began its descent into Brisbane, the familiar landscape of Queensland stretching out below him. After the adrenaline of the test in Italy, the transition back to normal life felt surreal. He could still feel the hum of the OKN-J kart beneath him, the way it demanded his complete focus, his nerves, his strength. Yet here he was, thousands of miles away from South Garda, heading home.

As they touched down, he felt a quiet buzz of excitement beneath the surface, tempered by the weight of what was coming next. He knew this was just the beginning. The test had been exhilarating, and now the door to junior racing was wide open, waiting for him to walk through.

Seb watched as his dad, Babak, checked his phone as soon as they were allowed to turn them back on. His father's face lit up, and Seb could see something had shifted.

"Joakim messaged," Babak said, turning to Kelly with a grin. "He wants Seb on the Ward Racing team for OKN-J for next year."

Seb's heart raced. He hadn't expected to hear so soon, but now that the offer was there, it was like everything he'd worked for was starting to fall into place. Yet, mixed in with his excitement was a flicker of uncertainty. This was a big step. Racing in OKN-J meant higher speeds, tougher competition, and more at stake.

"What do you think Seb?" Babak asked, as they walked through the airport towards baggage claim, his tone quiet but steady.

Seb paused for a moment, feeling the question sink in. He was excited—thrilled, even—but also aware of the pressure that came with moving up. "Yeah," he nodded, trying to sound as confident as he could. "I'm ready."

Back home, the days were a whirlwind of preparation as Seb returned to Ipswich Kart Track with a laser-sharp focus. His training was under the watchful eye of Peter Crossingham—or "Pete," as Seb fondly called him. Pete wasn't just a coach; he had been part of Seb's journey since the age of seven, evolving into both a close friend and a trusted mentor. Throughout the Australian Karting Championship, Pete's wisdom and experience had been an anchor for Seb. Whether it was a quick strategy adjustment between heats or a moment of encouragement after a tough race, Seb knew he could always count on Pete to guide him through.

Even during Seb's stint in Italy the previous year, their connection remained strong. Late-night phone calls became routine, filled with updates and virtual track walks over WhatsApp. Pete's steady voice carried a sense of familiarity that helped Seb navigate the challenges of competing abroad. Now, with the transition to junior racing on the horizon, Pete pushed Seb harder than ever. Every practice session, every drill, was a step toward refining Seb's skills and building his confidence. Pete understood just how much this next chapter meant to Seb, and he was determined to prepare him for the challenges that lay ahead.

"These karts are faster, Seb," Pete said, leaning over the kart after another intense practice session. "But it's not just about speed. You've got to stay sharp, keep your head in the game. You're going to be racing against older kids, more experienced ones too."

Seb wiped the sweat from his brow, adjusting his gloves as he processed Pete's words. "I know," he replied, his voice determined but laced with the weight of the responsibility he carried. "That's why I'm working harder than ever."

Pete gave him a nod of approval. "Good. You've got what it takes. Just remember, every lap is a chance to improve."

Seb nodded, taking the advice to heart. He'd always prided himself on his ability to learn quickly, and with Pete's help, he could feel himself growing into the new kart, the faster speeds, the more aggressive driving style. But with every lap, every tweak to the kart, Seb couldn't help but feel the unspoken pressure. This was his shot—his first step into the world of junior racing—and he didn't want to waste it.

Training wasn't just limited to the track. Seb's routine was relentless. He'd rise at 6 am, have a quick snack and make it to the gym by 6:45 a.m., his eyes still adjusting to the early morning light. Each session was a mix of weights, cardio, and endurance, pushing him harder than he'd thought possible. He'd return home for breakfast before jumping into his online classes, his day just beginning. By the time lunch rolled around, Seb was already mentally preparing for his afternoon on the simulator, where he'd practice lap after lap until his shoulders ached.

Evenings were spent at triathlon training, working on stamina and endurance, and by the time he finally settled in for dinner, he'd barely have enough energy to play a round of FIFA with his dad. But he did, and it was a quiet ritual that he looked forward to, a chance to unwind and connect before bed. It was a gruelling schedule, but Seb had learned to turn to the words of athletes he admired—legends like Mike Tyson and Michael Jordan. Their voices filled his headphones, echoing the same message: *Get up every day and work harder than everyone else.*

While Seb stayed singularly focused on his training, Babak wrestled with a different reality. Seb's growing success carried a heavy price—one that weighed on Babak's mind daily. Racing in Europe was a costly endeavour, and as much as he wanted to give Seb every chance to chase his dream, the financial strain was starting to feel overwhelming. His colleague's words echoed constantly in his mind: "He can't make it, can he? You just don't have the money."

One evening, after Seb had gone to bed, Babak sat alone at the kitchen table, mentally running the numbers for what felt like the hundredth time. Kelly entered quietly and sat across from him, sensing his unease.

"How are we going to make this work, Kelly?" he asked softly, his voice filled with concern. "We've already sacrificed so much... and now we're looking at another full season in Italy?"

They sat there in the quiet, each carrying the weight of the journey they'd embarked on for Seb, trying to find a way to keep his dream alive.

Babak sighed, rubbing his hands over his face. "I know. It's not easy. But Seb's got so much potential, Kel. He's worked so hard, and this is his chance. I can't take that away from him."

Kelly looked at him, her eyes filled with both pride and worry. "I'm proud of him too. But I don't want us to end up drowning in this."

They sat in silence for a moment, the weight of their decision pressing down on them. Babak knew she was right. But he also knew that Seb's talent and passion was something special—something that couldn't be ignored.

The cost wasn't the only barrier Seb faced. To race in Italy in the OKN-J class, he needed a junior racing license—a qualification reserved for drivers over the age of 12. But Seb was still only 10, and the rules felt like an insurmountable wall. Babak couldn't shake the feeling that this path was essential for Seb's growth, so the next day, with a mix of nerves and resolve, he picked up the phone and called Lee Hanatschek, the CEO of Karting Australia.

As Babak explained their unique situation, he laid out the vision he had for Seb—to make the leap to juniors early, which would open the door for him to race in Italy under his Australian National license. Babak's voice carried a hopeful determination, each word underscoring just how much this opportunity meant to Seb's future. Lee listened thoughtfully, recognizing the significance of the request, and asked Babak to submit a formal application for the panel's review.

Days turned into weeks, each one stretched thin with anticipation as they waited for an answer. Every time Babak refreshed his inbox, he felt his pulse quicken. Then, one quiet afternoon, the awaited email from Karting Australia finally arrived. Babak's heart raced as he clicked it open, his eyes scanning the lines until he found it: *Exemption granted.*

In that moment, all the obstacles, the hurdles, and the long wait faded away. This was more than just approval—it was a testament to Seb's hard work and Babak's belief in him.

When Babak told Seb the news, the young driver's eyes lit up. "Really? I can race in Italy now?" Seb's excitement was palpable, but Babak saw the determination beneath it.

"Yeah, you can," Babak said, smiling. "But it's going to take a lot of work, Seb. This isn't going to be easy."

Seb nodded, his face serious. "I know, Dad. I'm ready."

The weeks that followed were filled with intense training sessions at Ipswich Kart Track. Pete pushed Seb hard, helping him fine-tune his skills, making sure he was prepared for the level of competition he'd face in Italy. Seb thrived under the pressure, his focus sharpening with each lap.

One afternoon, after a particularly gruelling session, Pete pulled Seb aside. "You're getting faster, Seb," he said, his tone approving. "But remember, it's not just about speed. It's about consistency, tyre management and self-belief. When you're racing in Italy, there will be moments where you feel like giving up—where things don't go your way. That's when you have to dig deep."

Seb looked up at Pete, his eyes filled with determination. "I won't give up," he said quietly. "I've come too far to stop now."

As the weeks passed, Seb's confidence grew. He was getting faster, more consistent, and his love for racing burned brighter than ever. But beneath the surface, he knew the pressure was mounting—not just for him, but for his family too. Babak's quiet stress about the finances hadn't gone unnoticed, and though Seb didn't say anything, he carried the weight of that knowledge with him.

Still, Seb pushed forward, knowing that the only way to repay the sacrifices his family was making was to give everything he had on the track. With each practice session, each lap, he grew more confident, more ready for the next chapter in his racing career.

As the day of their return to Italy approached, Seb stood at the edge of the track at Ipswich, looking out over the asphalt. The sun was setting, casting a golden glow over the karts lined up in the pits. He felt a mixture of excitement and nerves as he thought about what was coming next. Italy was calling, and this time, he wasn't just testing the waters. He was stepping into the next phase of his journey.

He glanced over at his dad, who was standing nearby, watching him with a proud but thoughtful expression. Babak caught his eye and smiled.

"You happy?" Babak asked.

Seb nodded, feeling the weight of the moment, but also the excitement. "Yeah," he said softly, his heart racing with anticipation. "I'm ready."

And with that, the next chapter of Seb's journey began—one filled with challenges, but also with the promise of something great.

"FIRST RACE, FIRST CHALLENGE"

The crisp air of early April filled the Franciacorta circuit as Seb sat in his kart, gripping the steering wheel. The sound of engines roaring to life echoed around the track, the adrenaline building in his chest. This was his first race in the OKN-J class, and everything felt bigger, faster, and more intense than anything he'd experienced before. He had trained hard for this moment, but now that it was here, nerves tingled under his skin.

Beside him, Babak was looking over the kart, his face calm but focused. Franciacorta was known for its technical layout and aggressive competition. It wasn't going to be an easy race, but Seb knew he had the speed and skill to hold his own. What he wasn't sure about was how to handle the pressure—both from the other drivers and from within himself.

"You ready?" Babak asked, offering Seb a reassuring smile.

Seb nodded, though the butterflies in his stomach made it hard to speak. "Yeah, I'm ready." His voice was steadier than he felt, but he knew he had to keep it together. This wasn't just another race. This was the next level.

After arriving in Italy a few days earlier, they were greeted by familiar faces, but the biggest change had come in the form of Konstantin, Seb's new mechanic. He was an ex Russian rally driver, he had a presence without been imposing, with a no-nonsense demeanour... and a reputation for being tough but fair. Their relationship was still in its early stages, and Seb hadn't quite figured him out yet.

"Get in the kart," Konstantin had said that morning, his voice a little gruff. "We have work to do."

Seb followed instructions, settling into the seat and adjusting his gloves. He could feel Konstantin's eyes on him, scrutinizing every movement. The pressure was real, but as the engine roared to life, Seb's nerves started to melt away.

"Don't overthink it," Konstantin had told him, leaning down before the session. "Drive smart, drive fast. Stay calm. You know what to do."

Seb took that advice to heart. Lap after lap, he pushed himself, feeling out the kart's limits, and with each practice session, his times edged faster. By the end of the day, he noticed Konstantin giving him a small nod of approval. It wasn't much, but it was enough to tell Seb he was on the right track. At the end of the session, Seb asked, "So, are you happy with it?"

Konstantin gave a half-smile, shrugging slightly. "For me, it's okay," he replied in his usual reserved tone. "But I'll be happy when we're standing on the podium."

Now, on race day, Seb's thoughts swirled around everything that had led him to this moment. He had qualified 2nd in his group, just 0.005 seconds behind the fastest driver. That tiny margin stung, but Seb was proud of himself. He was the youngest driver in the OKN-J class, racing against kids who had been doing this for years. The fact that he was even this close to the front was a win in itself.

As he lined up for the first heat, the weight of the competition began to settle in. These drivers weren't just fast—they were ruthless. Seb had seen it in their eyes, the way they sized him up, knowing he was younger, perhaps expecting him to fold under the pressure.

The lights went out, and the karts shot forward. Seb held his ground, gripping the wheel tightly as they barrelled into the first corner. The jostling began almost immediately, elbows out, tires bumping, and karts pushing for position. It was chaotic, and Seb quickly realized that this wasn't like the racing he was used to.

By the end of the first heat, Seb had dropped back to 17th. It wasn't the start he had hoped for, and frustration bubbled beneath the surface. But there was no time to dwell on it. The second heat came quickly, and this time, Seb was ready for the rough driving. He fought harder, holding his lines, and clawed his way up to 5th.

Konstantin didn't say much when Seb returned to the tent after the second heat, just handed him a bottle of water. But there was a flicker of something in his eyes—something like approval.

"You did better," Konstantin said, his words clipped but encouraging. "But you can do more."

Seb nodded, already replaying the race in his head, thinking about what he could have done differently. The third heat was just as intense, and Seb ended up finishing 10th after a tough battle in the midfield. He wasn't where he wanted to be, but he knew he was learning with every lap.

That night, as they sat in the hotel room, Babak turned to Seb, his voice soft. "You're doing great, Seb. This is a tough field, and you're holding your own. Just keep pushing."

Seb sighed, leaning back against the headboard. "It's harder than I thought, Dad. The way they drive... it's like they don't care if they hit you."

Babak nodded. "That's the game at this level. You have to stay calm, stay focused. You're just as fast as they are, maybe faster. You've proven that already."

Seb stared at the ceiling, the weight of the competition pressing down on him. But beneath it all, there was a flicker of excitement. He was here, racing at the highest level for his age, and despite the challenges, he was holding his own.

The next day brought the pre-final. Seb started 10th on the grid, determined to make up ground. As the race began, he fought his way through the field, overtaking with precision and confidence. By the time the chequered flag waved, he had climbed up to 7th. It wasn't a podium, but it was progress, and that was what mattered.

As Seb pulled into the pits, Konstantin was there, arms crossed but a faint smile tugging at the corners of his mouth. "Not bad, Seb. Not bad at all."

The final race was the culmination of everything Seb had been working for. He lined up in 9th, surrounded by older, more experienced drivers. The tension was thick in the air as the engines roared to life. Seb's heart raced, but his mind was clear. He knew what he had to do.

The race was a battle from the start. Seb fought hard, trading positions, defending his line, and pushing his kart to the limit. The corners came fast, and the straights felt like a blur, but Seb was in the zone. He knew he had the speed—he just needed to stay focused.

Lap after lap, he chipped away at the drivers in front of him, working his way up the field. By the final laps, he was running in 5th, holding off a hard-charging group behind him. The chequered flag waved, and Seb crossed the line, his heart pounding with a mix of relief and pride.

He had done it. His first race in the OKN-J class, and he had finished 5th. It wasn't a win, but it felt like one.

As he climbed out of the kart, Babak was there, a wide grin on his face. "You did it, Seb!" Babak pulled him into a hug, pride radiating from every word. "You proved yourself today."

Seb smiled, the weight of the weekend lifting off his shoulders. "Yeah," he said, his voice soft but filled with determination. "I did."

Later that day, as they packed up, Mr. Robazzi, the owner of Tony Kart, stopped by the Ward Racing tent. His eyes twinkled with approval as he approached Seb and Babak.

"You've done well," Mr. Robazzi said, his tone warm. "You have a bright future ahead of you."

Seb's chest swelled with pride. Hearing that from someone like Mr. Robazzi felt like a dream. It wasn't just about today's race—it was about everything that lay ahead.

As they loaded Seb's gear bag into the trunk of the car, Babak turned to Seb. "You know we have a big year ahead of us."

Seb glanced back at the track, the place where he had faced his first real challenge in this new class, and smiled. "Yeah, I know." he said, his voice steady. "I'm looking forward to it."

The sun began to set over Franciacorta, casting long shadows across the now-quiet track. Seb stood there for a moment, taking it all in. This was just the beginning, and he knew the road ahead would be tough. But for the first time, he felt like he truly belonged here. And that was enough. For now.

"HOMECOMING AND TRIUMPH AT IPSWICH"

Seb stepped off the plane and took a deep breath of the warm Queensland air, a wave of familiarity washing over him. After the intensity of his first race in Italy, being home felt grounding. The brightness of the Queensland sky, and the comforting hum of life back in Brisbane reminded him of the simpler days when karting was just something fun he did on weekends. But now, everything felt different. The track that had once been his playground was now part of his journey to something much bigger, and stepping back onto home soil carried a weight he hadn't anticipated.

The decision to race in the junior classes at Ipswich hadn't come right away. Babak and Seb spent the first couple of weeks settling back in—catching up with family, reconnecting with friends, and finding moments of calm in between. Seb relished being home, eating Kelly's home-cooked meals and sleeping in his own bed, the little comforts he'd missed during his time away.

But the track called to him. Practice sessions at Ipswich soon became a daily ritual, as Seb reacquainted himself with the curves and straights of a place that had once been second nature. Each lap brought a flood of memories, from his earliest races to the milestones that had paved the way to Italy. This wasn't just practice; it was a homecoming.

By the time they committed to entering the race weekend, Seb felt ready. It would be his first time competing in KA3 and KA2 on home soil, and the significance of returning to Ipswich wasn't lost on him. He hadn't raced there for almost two years, and the thought of competing in front of old friends and familiar faces brought a mix of excitement and pressure. But Seb was no stranger to pressure. As the weekend approached, he focused on preparation, fine-tuning his skills, and drawing confidence from the place that had shaped the driver he was becoming. The next chapter of his journey was about to unfold, and Ipswich was the perfect place to begin.

For Babak, however, the weekend carried a different kind of weight. It had been a while since he'd served as Seb's mechanic, and with the new karts and engines, he couldn't help but feel a little rusty. But, as always, their racing family came through. Pete Crossingham had generously offered Seb a spot in his team tent, providing engines and the support of a seasoned mechanic, Jason Platten. Jason's son wasn't racing that weekend, and he'd volunteered to step in. His meticulous nature and easy going personality quickly made an impression on both Seb and Babak.

"It's been a while since I've done this," Babak admitted with a laugh as he handed Jason a set of tools.

Jason smiled warmly. "Don't worry, mate. We've got this. Seb's in good hands."

Seb, meanwhile, felt a surge of excitement as he reunited with friends he hadn't seen in years. Laughter and stories filled the paddock, but as qualifying approached, his focus sharpened. This wasn't just a fun homecoming—it was a chance to prove himself in the junior class.

Seb rolled onto the track for KA3 qualifying, the buzz of anticipation hanging in the air. As the kart roared to life beneath him, he eased into the session, letting the machine settle into a rhythm that felt natural. With each passing lap, Seb's confidence grew—his lines were smooth, his braking points sharp, and every corner flowed seamlessly into the next. As the session came to an end, his time was clear. Pole position was his.

Later in KA2 qualifying, Seb delivered another flawless performance, when the session ended, he had secured pole position again with a gap that left his competitors shaking their heads. Pete gave him a nod of approval as Seb climbed out of the kart.

"Well done," Pete said, his tone calm but proud. "Now, remember what we talked about—tyre management. It'll make all the difference in the finals."

Seb nodded, his eyes shining with determination. "Got it, Pete. Thanks."

The KA3 heat one marked Seb's first race of the weekend, and it was already shaping up to be a test of strategy and skill. Starting the event with high expectations, he faced a tough challenge in the first heat. Despite his best efforts, Seb crossed the line in second place, the kart feeling slightly off in balance as he experienced a fair bit of oversteer. Back in the pits, Pete offered calm guidance, helping Seb and the team make a few adjustments.

"Focus on the bigger picture," Pete reminded him, his voice steady. "The heats are important, but the final is where it counts. Stay smooth, save the tyres, and trust your instincts."

The adjustments paid off. In the second heat, Seb found his rhythm. Starting from pole, he took the lead from the start of the race with a sharp, calculated move, and from there, he controlled the pace. By the time the chequered flag waved, Seb had claimed victory, setting him up perfectly for the final.

When the final began, Seb was laser-focused. Starting from pole, he surged into the first corner, fending off challenges from the pack behind him. Pete's advice about tyre saving echoed in his mind as he maintained a smooth, calculated pace. While the competition battled fiercely for position behind him, Seb concentrated on preserving his tyres, ensuring he'd have the edge in the closing laps. The kart felt like an extension of himself, every turn precise, every decision deliberate.

By the time he crossed the finish line, Seb had pulled ahead by an impressive 4.1 seconds, claiming victory and setting the fastest lap of the race. As he slowed down and pulled into the pits, the familiar roar of the Ipswich crowd filled the air, a wave of nostalgia washing over him. Seb couldn't help but smile. It felt incredible to be back on his home track, not just racing, but winning.

The KA2 final brought Seb's weekend to a satisfying close. Having already won both heats earlier in the day with steady, calculated driving, he approached the final with quiet determination. Each heat had been a test of consistency, and Seb's focus on smooth, tyre-preserving laps had paid off, allowing him to manage the races from the front.

As the green lights signalled the start of the final, Seb made a clean getaway, holding his position at the front as the pack jostled for places behind him. Settling into a rhythm, he concentrated on maintaining his lines and keeping his driving smooth, just as Pete had reminded him. By the midpoint of the race, he had opened a comfortable gap. On the straight, Pete and Babak gestured to him to stay calm and avoid overdriving. Seb nodded inwardly, easing into a steadier pace, yet to his surprise, his lap times improved as he drove more smoothly.

The laps ticked by, and Seb's kart felt like an extension of himself, responding to every nudge of the wheel and press of the pedal. By the time the chequered flag waved, Seb crossed the line 3.4 seconds ahead of his nearest rival, securing his second final win of the weekend and the fastest lap of the race. The victory wasn't just about speed; it was a showcase of focus, control, and the teamwork that had supported him throughout.

Pulling into the pits, Seb climbed out of his kart, greeted by Pete and Babak, their smiles reflecting the pride they felt. "That was excellent driving, Seb," Pete said, giving him a firm pat on the shoulder. "You stayed calm, and it paid off."

Babak nodded in agreement. "You handled it well—smooth and smart."

Seb returned their smiles, his gloves dangling from his hand. "It felt good out there. I just tried to focus on what we talked about."

It had been a weekend filled with lessons, growth, and a chance to race at home again. Ipswich, the track where so many of his first memories were made, had welcomed him back with a reminder of how far he'd come—and how much further he could still go.

After the podium celebrations, Seb found himself surrounded by friends, old and new, sharing stories and laughter in the paddock. It was more than just a race weekend—it was a homecoming, a chance to reconnect with the people and places that had shaped his journey.

As they packed up that evening, Babak placed a hand on Seb's shoulder. "This weekend was special," he said, his voice filled with pride. "You've come a long way, Seb."

Seb smiled, his mind already drifting to Italy and the challenges that lay ahead. But for now, he allowed himself to savour the moment. Ipswich had reminded him of where he'd come from, but it also showed him just how far he could go.

44

TONY KART
44
EMPIRE

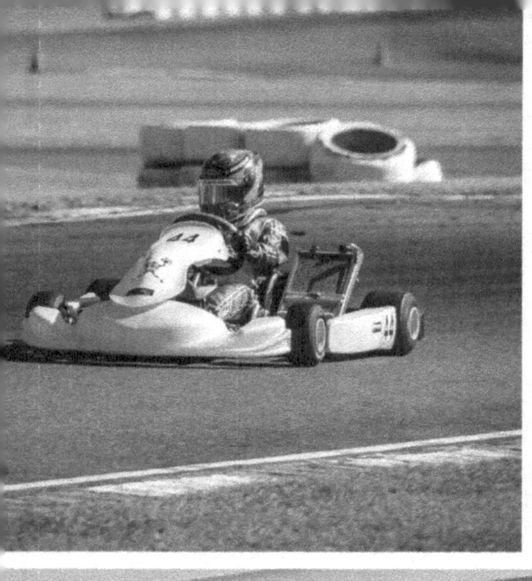

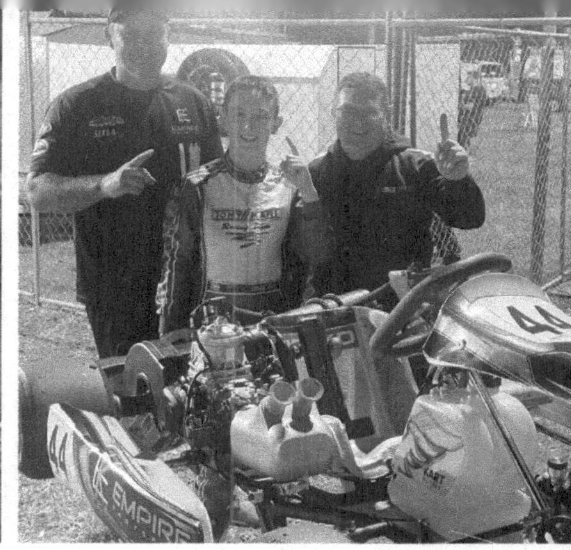

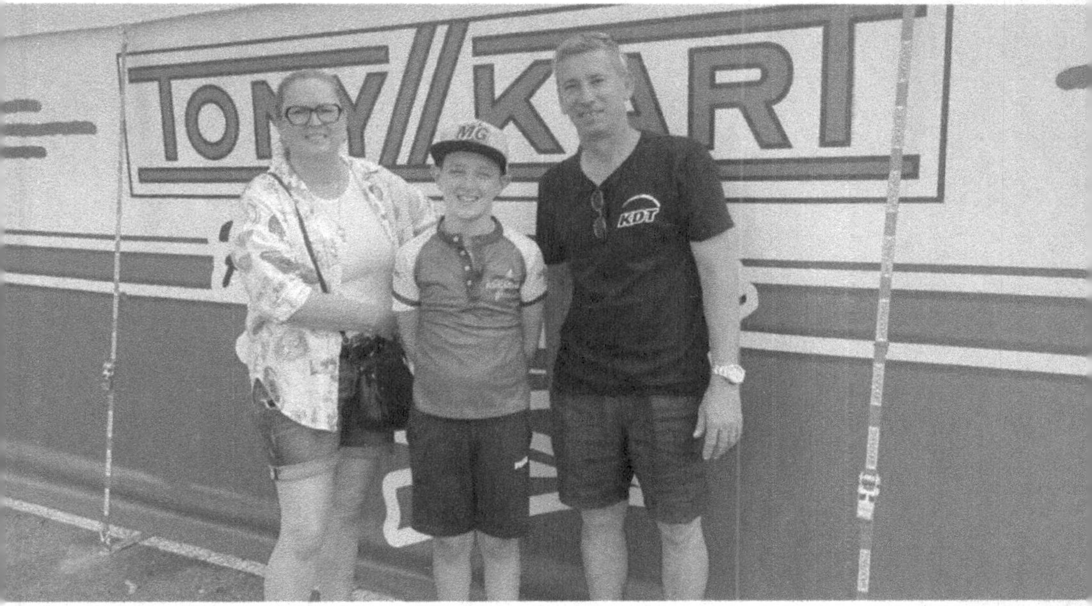
TONY KART
MG
KDT

LB
TONY KART

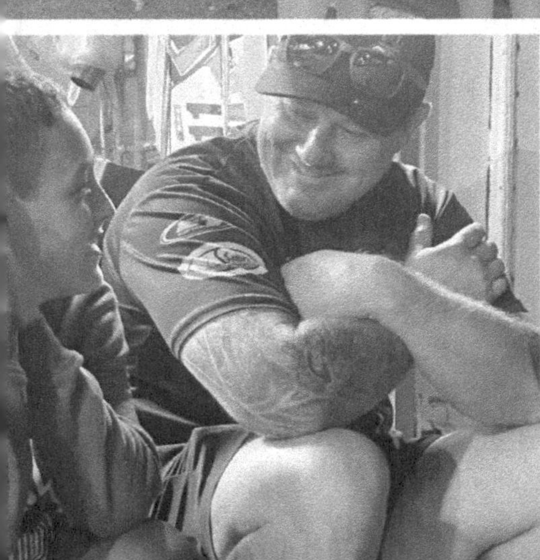

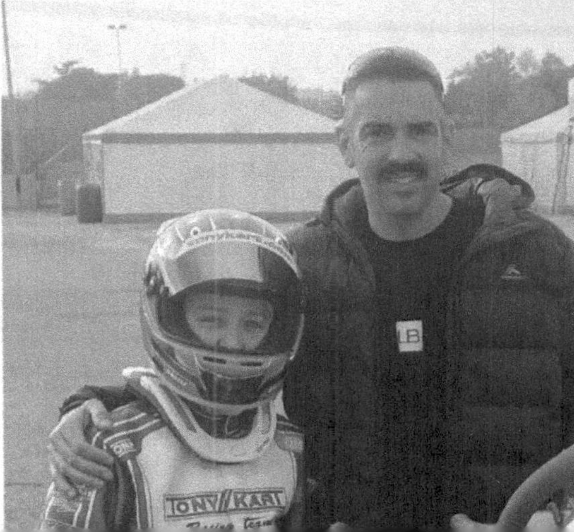

"PODIUM BREAKTHROUGH"

Sebastian stood at the edge of the La Conca track, the familiar hum of engines in the background filling the air. This wasn't his first time in Italy, but it felt different—more significant. His dad wasn't here this time; it was just him and his mom, Kelly, who had travelled across the world for his next challenge. Babak had stayed back in Australia, handling work, while Seb and Kelly navigated the Italian racing scene on their own. The distance was hard, but Seb knew his dad would be watching, following every lap, every corner, from home, after all he had done it the year before.

It had been a whirlwind since their return from Australia. After his first race in Franciacorta, Seb had flown back home, where he had spent weeks training and preparing. The test sessions, the early mornings at Ipswich Kart Track, everything had led to this—the second round of the Italian Kart Championship. La Conca was known for its fast-paced, technical corners, and Seb could feel the excitement pulsing in his veins. But without his dad's usual presence, there was an unfamiliar quiet, a different kind of pressure hanging in the air.

"Ready?" Kelly asked, standing beside him as they waited for his turn to qualify. Her voice was soft, her smile full of encouragement, but Seb could see the underlying nerves she was trying to hide. She had always been his rock, but the absence of his dad created a small gap neither of them knew quite how to fill.

Seb nodded, adjusting his gloves and helmet. "Yeah, I'm ready."

He could feel the anticipation building, both within himself and the paddock around him. This was a big moment—another chance to prove himself after the two rounds of the WSK Open series where he had finished 5th and 6th respectively. He had shown promise, but a podium had eluded him so far. Today, that could change.

As he climbed into the kart, Seb's mind zeroed in on the task at hand. The familiar sounds of the track and the weight of the kart beneath him brought a sense of calm. Everything else—the distance from home, the absence of his dad—faded away. It was just him, the kart, and the track.

The qualifying laps were tense. Seb pushed himself hard, every ounce of focus channelled into the kart's response as it weaved through each turn and powered down the straights. Unlike his competitors, Seb chose to go out alone, deliberately avoiding the tow others relied on for extra speed. It wasn't about proving a point—it was about trust. Seb believed in his own pace, confident in the countless hours he'd spent honing his skill. He didn't need the slipstream of another kart to boost his time.

The track was slick, every turn demanding precision and every straight requiring perfect control. But Seb was locked in, his body and mind moving in flawless sync with the machine beneath him. The kart responded to his touch as if it were an extension of himself, slicing through the challenging conditions with unrelenting focus. Each lap felt like a battle against the clock, every corner an opportunity to prove his skill.

As he crossed the line, the results flashed on the board—2nd fastest in the quickest group, 3rd overall. A flicker of pride lit up his chest. He'd done it on his own terms, with no assistance, just raw determination and trust in his ability. But Seb wasn't one to linger on achievements for long. He was the pole sitter for Group C, which meant starting from position 2—the tricky outside line—for both upcoming heats. The real challenge was just beginning, and Seb could feel the energy building within him. He was ready to take it on.

In the first heat race, Seb lined up on the grid in 2nd, next to a 13-year-old Russian driver who had one and half more years of experience in the junior class. The tension was electric as the karts rolled toward the start line. The Russian driver slowed the pack to a crawl, forcing Seb to hold back, careful not to jump the start. When the green lights finally flashed, the race was on—but Seb found himself crossing the start line in 4th, caught off guard by the sluggish rollout.

The opening turns were a chaotic blur. Two fast right-handers led into a sharp right hairpin, and the jostling pack shuffled Seb down to 17th by the exit of the corner. His frustration flared, but he quickly channelled it into focus. "One lap at a time," he told himself, his hands tightening on the wheel. By the end of the first lap, Seb had clawed back two positions, sitting in 15th with 11 laps to go.

He pushed hard, finding every possible gap and taking calculated risks in the corners. By the fourth lap, he'd surged up to 10th, but the gap to 9th was over a second. Undeterred, he settled into a rhythm, shaving tenths off his lap times with each pass around the circuit. By lap 7, he was right on the bumper of 9th place. His focus sharpened, and over the next few laps, Seb executed four clean overtakes, moving up to 6th as the final lap approached.

As he crossed the finish line, Seb's chest heaved with exhaustion, but his heart soared. He had fought his way back from 17th to 6th, setting the fastest lap of the race in the process. It wasn't a win, but it was a statement. Climbing out of the kart, he spotted Kelly running toward him, her face lit with pride.

"You were amazing!" she exclaimed, pulling him into a quick hug.

Seb grinned, pulling off his helmet. "Thanks, Mom. That was tough, but I felt good out there."

His heart was still racing, but beneath it all, there was a calm satisfaction. He'd proven that even in the face of a tough start, he could fight his way back. There was more work to be done, but Seb was ready for whatever came next.

In the second heat race, Seb was back in P2, this time lining up alongside a confident 14-year-old Italian driver. The tension on the grid was palpable, but Seb's mind was steady. The start was smoother than the first heat, the pace more consistent. When the green light flashed, Seb surged forward, crossing the start line in 3rd. Navigating the first three right-hand turns, he carefully slotted into P4, biding his time.

The pack began to spread out, and Seb saw his opportunity. By lap 2, he made his move into 3rd, smoothly overtaking on the inside of a sharp turn. The leading pair were about eight-tenths ahead, their karts pulling away on the straights. Seb gritted his teeth and pushed harder, finding the limits of his kart in every corner. By the end of lap 4, he was right on their tail.

Lap 5 was his moment. Coming out of a sweeping right-hander, Seb powered past the second-place driver, claiming 2nd and setting his sights on the leader. The gap was a steady seven-tenths, but Seb's pace was relentless. Lap after lap, he chipped away at the lead, his kart carving through the technical sections with precision.

By lap 9, Seb was on the leader's bumper, his heart pounding with anticipation. "Patience," he reminded himself, waiting for the perfect moment. It came on lap 10, as the leader left a small gap entering a hairpin. Seb dived through, his kart sliding cleanly into the lead. With two laps to go, he maintained a flawless rhythm, keeping the chasing pack at bay.

As the chequered flag waved, Seb crossed the line seven-tenths ahead of the Italian driver, a triumphant grin spreading across his face. This wasn't just any win—it was his first victory in OKN-J, a milestone that felt as sweet as it was hard-earned.

Climbing out of the kart, Seb felt the weight of the moment. Kelly was waiting, her smile wide and filled with pride.

"That's how it's done, Seb," Kelly said, clapping him on the shoulder.

Seb nodded, his excitement barely contained, the joy of his first OKN-J win lighting up his face.

It was a win that marked not just progress but a glimpse of what lay ahead. Seb was proving he belonged in this new class.

The first final arrived, and Seb could feel the weight of the moment. This was the bigger of the two finals—new tires, more championship points, and a chance to prove himself in OKN-J. He was starting from P3, expecting to line up behind the Russian driver who had dominated much of the weekend. But a pre-race rain had left parts of the track damp, particularly the inside line leading into the first fast right-hander. The pole sitter took advantage of the rules, choosing to start from the drier, outside racing line. It left Seb on the damp side, a disadvantage he hadn't anticipated.

As the karts rolled onto the grid and the green lights flashed, Seb surged forward. Despite his determination, the damp track caught him out, and by the time he crossed the start line, he had slipped to 6th. Through the chaotic scramble of the opening lap, Seb found himself down in 8th, frustration bubbling beneath his calm exterior. But he refused to let it consume him.

"Keep your head, Seb," he told himself, gripping the wheel tighter as the laps unfolded.

By the end of lap 3, Seb had climbed back to 5th, picking off drivers with calculated moves and precision through the technical sections. The kart felt strong beneath him, and Seb used every ounce of its potential. Lap by lap, he clawed his way through the field. By lap 7, he was in 3rd, his sights now set on the front runners.

Just as he began to close the gap to second place, a full-course yellow was called, freezing the field for three laps. Seb exhaled deeply, trying to keep his focus as the karts slowed behind the leader.

When the green flag waved at the start of lap 11, Seb seized his opportunity. As they charged into the first fast right-hander, he made his move, darting to the inside and taking 2nd with a clean, decisive pass. The leader was a second ahead, but Seb was relentless, pushing harder with each lap. By the time they approached the front straight to start the final lap, Seb was right on the leader's bumper.

He lined up his move perfectly, diving to the inside as they barrelled down the straight at 120 km/hr. The Russian glanced over, then veered toward Seb, squeezing him hard to the inside. Seb didn't flinch. He held his line, his kart just inches from the grass, and edged ahead into turn one.

"I've got this," Seb thought, adrenaline coursing through him.

But as they approached turn three, a sharp hairpin, Seb made a small miscalculation. He only half-covered the inside line, leaving just enough space for the Russian to dive through. The move was aggressive, but within the limits. Seb had no choice but to concede the position. For the rest of the lap, the Russian blocked every attempt Seb made to overtake, leaving him with no openings.

As they crossed the finish line, Seb took 2nd place, just a tenth behind. It wasn't the win he'd hoped for, but as he pulled into the pits, Kelly was already waiting, her face filled with pride.

"That was incredible, Seb," she said, pulling him into a hug. "You raced like a champion out there."

Seb climbed out of the kart, his chest still heaving from the effort but a small smile breaking through. "I thought I had him," he said.

"You'll get him next time," Kelly said, her voice warm. "This is just the beginning."

Seb nodded. This was his first podium in an OKN-J final—a milestone in his journey. The disappointment of the near-win couldn't overshadow the pride of how far he'd come.

The second final loomed, and Seb could feel the weight of the challenge ahead. With the top eight grid positions reversed, he was starting from 7th. It wasn't going to be easy, but Seb thrived in tough races. This was his chance to prove himself again.

As he lined up on the grid, Seb glanced down the row of karts, the tension in the air almost tangible. He tightened his grip on the steering wheel, his mind running through the race strategy. He knew what he had to do: stay calm, pick his moments, and push harder than ever. The lights turned green and then they were off.

Seb launched, his kart surging forward as the engines roared around him. The start was chaotic, but Seb's instincts were sharp. By the time he crossed the start line, he had already climbed to

5th. Through the twists and turns of the opening lap, Seb continued to push, finding gaps and taking calculated risks. As the first lap ended, he had moved up to 4th, his determination unshaken.

The second lap brought even more precision. Seb zeroed in on the kart ahead, taking advantage of a late braking zone to claim 3rd. Each move was smooth, calculated, and relentless. By the end of lap 3, Seb was in 2nd, his focus locked on the leader. He could feel the kart beneath him, responsive and powerful, and with every corner, his confidence grew.

Lap 4 was his moment. Seb saw the opportunity and didn't hesitate. Coming out of a fast left-hand corner, he slid to the inside of the leader for the right hand hairpin, executing a clean, decisive pass. The move was flawless, and now, the race was his to control.

From that point forward, Seb was untouchable—or so it seemed. By the end of lap 5, he noticed something alarming: the fuel line going from the tank to the breather tank had come loose, leaking fuel. On lap 6, he made a split-second decision to hold the fuel line in his hand while driving, keeping it steady to minimize the leak. The fuel began to leak onto his glove. The sharp, stinging sensation of the fuel burning his hand hit immediately, but Seb stayed focused. Each lap became a battle, not just against the track but against the discomfort and the growing sting in his hand.

Despite the burning pain, Seb's focus never wavered. Lap after lap, he extended his lead, the gap between him and the pack growing with each turn. His kart seemed to dance on the track, perfectly in sync with his every command, even as his hand throbbed with each passing second. By the time he crossed the finish line, Seb had pulled away to win by an impressive 3.3 seconds, the victory hard-earned and unforgettable.

The crowd roared as Seb slowed down and pulled into the pits, the noise ringing in his ears. For a moment, he just sat in his kart, his chest heaving, the enormity of what he'd accomplished starting to sink in—his first victory in an OKN-J final, his first major triumph in the category. But beneath the rush of adrenaline, a knot of worry coiled in his stomach. The fuel line issue loomed large in his mind—had he lost too much fuel? Would he be underweight and face disqualification?

As the officials waved him over to the scales, Seb's heart pounded harder than it had during the race. He climbed out of the kart and watched as it was weighed. The seconds felt like an eternity until the number popped up on the screen—he'd made weight. Relief flooded through him, and a small, triumphant grin spread across his face. The win was his, fair and square, and the weight of the worry lifted as he stepped away from the scales, his confidence soaring.

Konstantin was the first to reach him, his face lit up with pride. Without hesitation, he scooped Seb up in a big hug, his voice filled with excitement. "You did it! Your first final win in OKN-J—and the fastest lap of the weekend!"

Seb laughed, still catching his breath as he pulled off his helmet, his hair damp with sweat. "Thanks, Konstantin. I can't believe it," he said, his voice tinged with a mix of disbelief and pride. The adrenaline still coursed through him, the magnitude of what he'd just accomplished slowly sinking in.

Kelly arrived next, her eyes glistening with tears of joy as she wrapped him in a tight hug. "You were amazing out there," she said, her voice trembling with emotion. "You've worked so hard for this, and now look at you!"

Seb grinned, his chest swelling with pride, but his thoughts drifted to the one person who wasn't there—his dad. Kelly pulled out her phone and handed it to him with a knowing smile.

The line connected, and Babak's voice came through, brimming with pride. "Sebby! I watched the whole thing—you were incredible, mate! A win. That's awesome. I'm so proud of you."

Seb's grin widened as he listened to his dad's words. "Thanks, Dad. I just kept pushing. I wanted this so bad."

"I know you did," Babak replied, his voice steady and full of conviction. "And you earned it. This is just the beginning, Seb. Keep doing what you're doing, and the sky's the limit."

As Seb hung up the phone, he looked around at the bustling paddock, the roar of engines in the background. This wasn't just a win; it was a defining moment—a step forward into a future he could now see more clearly.

As Seb stood on the podium, the weight of the trophy in his hands, he looked out over the track. The cheers from the crowd were still ringing in his ears, but his thoughts were already on the next race. This was just the beginning. There were more challenges ahead, more races to win, but for now, Seb let himself bask in the moment.

That night, back at the apartment, Seb lay in bed. His body was tired, but his mind was racing. He thought about his dad, halfway across the world, watching his race. He wished Babak had been there to see it first-hand. But Seb knew his dad was proud, even from a distance. They were a team, no matter where they were in the world.

Kelly knocked on the doorframe, leaning in. "Proud of you, Seb," she said softly.

"Thanks, Mom," Seb replied, his voice quiet.

As she left the room, Seb took one last look at the trophy sitting on the table. He had earned it—through hard work, determination, and grit. And as he closed his eyes, he knew that this was just the first of many. There were bigger victories ahead.

"SETBACKS AND SURGES"

Seb sat quietly, his gaze fixed on the rolling Italian countryside as it blurred past. The endless rows of vineyards and rustic farmhouses flashed by, but his mind was elsewhere, tangled in the memories of the past few weeks. It had been a whirlwind of triumphs and frustrations, each moment as sharp and vivid as the next, creating a season that was proving to be his hardest yet. He knew racing was a game of highs and lows, but this? This felt like an uphill climb he hadn't expected, each setback leaving a lingering sense of unfinished business that gnawed at him.

The midseason races had pushed Seb in ways he hadn't expected, each weekend unfolding with its own unique challenge.

Val Vibrata was a track Seb had always liked. Its technical corners suited his style, and after 3 days of testing, he felt ready. His qualifying time had been strong—he was right up there with the fastest drivers, and things seemed to be lining up for a solid race weekend. But as soon as the heats began, the unpredictability of karting hit him hard.

Seb was on track, feeling the kart hum beneath him, he was in second position and challenging for the win with 4 corners to go on the final lap, when the engine sputtered, then died completely. He coasted to a stop, heart sinking as karts zipped past him. An engine failure. A DNF in the first heat.

Walking back in the pits, helmet in hand, feeling a wave of disappointment wash over him. Konstantin, his Russian mechanic, was already inspecting the engine.

"Just bad luck," Konstantin muttered, shaking his head. "A bolt on the timing mechanism. Nothing you could've done."

Seb gave a small nod, biting back his frustration. He knew it wasn't anyone's fault, but that didn't make it any easier. Karting was a sport where milliseconds mattered, and one tiny mechanical issue could ruin an entire race. But there was still time to turn things around. The final was coming up, and Seb was determined to bounce back.

The second heat went well so when the first final came up, Seb was starting from 14th. Starting on the outside saw him drop to 18th after turn one but Seb fought his way through the pack, each overtake a reminder of why he loved racing. By the time he crossed the finish line, he had clawed his way up to 9th. Not ideal, but a solid recovery. In the second final, starting from 9th, Seb found his groove. His kart felt perfect, and as he pushed through the field, he managed to finish 3rd—a podium, a satisfactory result despite the early setback of the weekend.

As he stood on the podium, looking out at the crowd, Seb felt a flicker of pride. It wasn't the win he had hoped for, but it was proof that he could fight back from anything.

Round 1 of the **WSK Euro Series at Franciacorta** was next, and this time, things started off even rougher. Seb qualified 2nd, just a whisper behind the pole sitter, but his luck took a turn during the formation lap of the first heat. His kart wouldn't accelerate. He hoped the carbi would clear and that it would sort itself out, but as he approached the uphill portion of sector one, it slowed, and stopped altogether.

Seb pulled off the track, heart sinking. He knew what this meant. Another DNF.

Konstantin met him back at the pits, a frown etched deep into his face. "Technical issue. Again."

Seb sighed, leaning against the kart. "I felt it right away. It just wouldn't go."

"You did the right thing, pulling off," Konstantin said, his voice softening. "It happens. You'll get them in the next heat."

And he did. In the next heat, Seb found his rhythm, driving like he had something to prove, and crossed the line a clear three and a half seconds ahead. For a moment, it felt like everything had finally clicked. But karting had its own way of humbling even the best drivers. In the third heat, just as he rolled out of the pits, he felt the all-too-familiar sputter of the carburettor acting up. Panic pricked at him, but he didn't hesitate—he stopped on the pit exit and pushed the kart back into the pits, his breaths quick and focused.

The pit crew worked fast, fixing the issue, and soon, Seb was back on the track, gunning it to catch up with the field. He pushed harder than he ever had, closing the gap, eyes locked on the red formation line. But as he reached it, he was just a meter too late, slipping into position a heartbeat after the line. Frustration flared, but he set it aside, throwing everything he had into the race. He crossed the finish line first, with a three-second lead. But then came the sting of the penalty—a five-second addition for his late position, dropping him to 6th.

Starting the pre-final in 6th, Seb knew he'd have to fight. He took the outside, but by the end of turns one and two, he'd fallen to 8th, the crowd of karts pushing him wide. Frustration simmered, but he fought his way back, clawing his way through the pack. He crossed the line in 3rd, only to be hit with another post-race penalty for minor contact, sliding him back to 6th again. The constant swings—up, down, close to glory, then snatched back—were exhausting, gnawing at his confidence. But he clenched his fists, breathing through the frustration. He wasn't about to let it break him.

Seb wasn't about to let anything stop him now. In the final, starting from 12th and forced to the outside again, he found himself dropping back to 15th as the pack thundered ahead. Gritting his teeth, he pushed hard, feeling every ounce of determination fuel his drive. This wasn't just about positions anymore; it was about proving he could claw his way back, no matter how far down he fell.

With every turn, every pass, he edged closer to the front, weaving his way through the field. The penalties, the setbacks—they were a blur behind him. All that mattered was the track ahead. Lap by lap, he closed in, feeling the momentum shift in his favour. By the final stretch, Seb crossed the line in 6th, the fastest lap of the race under his belt. He might not have taken the podium, but he'd won something else—the reminder that he could rise, no matter how many times he got knocked down.

Afterwards, back in the tent, Kelly smiled at him, pride written all over her face. "You're fighting through it," she said. "That's what counts."

Seb nodded, wiping the sweat from his forehead. "I just want a clean weekend."

Sarno was supposed to be that weekend. From the first practice session, Seb was unstoppable. He was the fastest in every session, and when qualifying came, he put it on pole—by over half a second. It was his first pole in OKN-J, and the margin was almost unheard of.

But karting, once again, had other plans. Before the heats began, Seb was issued a grid penalty for slowing down too much in qualifying. Neither he nor the team had been informed until the last minute, and suddenly, his pole position vanished. He would be starting 4th.

Seb was frustrated, but he didn't let it rattle him. He took the lead on lap two and pulled away, winning the heat by over two seconds. The second heat was just as smooth, another dominant win.

But when the first final came, disaster struck. As Seb powered through the first few laps, he noticed his engine temperature spiking. On lap three, the engine seized completely, sending him into a spin. It was another DNF.

Konstantin inspected the kart afterward, finding small stones in the water pump. "Closed circuit system," he muttered. "Shouldn't have happened."

Seb didn't say much, but the frustration was there, just beneath the surface. In the second final, he had to start on the second last row in 34th. As the karts lined up, he could feel the tension in the air. He was determined to salvage something from this weekend.

But karting can be cruel. As they came onto the front straight, the kart behind him ran into him, spinning Seb out before the race had even begun. His kart was damaged. His race was over.

Despite the setbacks, Seb refused to be defeated. Each race weekend seemed to throw new challenges his way, but he was learning to navigate them with grit and determination. The podiums he earned were hard-fought, but even the races where he didn't finish taught him something valuable.

Konstantin, once stoic and hard to read, had become one of Seb's biggest supporters. After a particularly tough race, he pulled Seb aside, his gaze steady. "You've got what it takes," he told him. "Keep pushing and stay calm. The results will come."

And Seb believed him. Racing was about much more than wins or trophies—it was about resilience, about fighting through the bad days and making the most of the good ones. The setbacks were frustrating, yes, but Seb could feel them shaping him into the driver he needed to be.

It wasn't just Konstantin who had his back. Rebecca Ward, Joakim's daughter, had become a familiar and comforting presence in Seb's racing life. On his first test day in the OKN-J at South Garda Kart Track, Seb met her, and from that moment, Rebecca was a source of energy and warmth in the paddock. Tall, with an easy smile, she'd greet Seb with a big, genuine hug every time she saw him. Most weekends, it was just him and Konstantin, but whenever the full Ward Racing team gathered, Rebecca's presence brought a sense of comfort and joy to their space. She would bring snacks, drinks, and her infectious laughter, filling the tent with a sense of family that made it feel like a home away from home.

Rebecca had a way of making Seb feel seen, understood, and appreciated. Her support extended to his whole family, and over the season, she became a friend he could rely on, someone who genuinely cared about his journey. Knowing she was cheering him on made even the toughest race days feel a little lighter.

As the season rolled on, Seb felt a growing sense of purpose. This journey wasn't over yet—not by a long shot.

"THE FINAL PUSH – FIVE WEEKS OF GLORY"

Sebastian felt the familiar weight of his racing helmet as he adjusted it one last time before stepping onto the track at Franciacorta. The morning air was crisp, the Italian breeze brushing past him as the early light of dawn painted the horizon. This was it—five intense weeks of racing stood between him and the end of the season. Four races to prove, once and for all, that he belonged on the world stage. His dad, Babak, would only be joining for the last two weeks, so for now, it was just him and his mom, Kelly.

He turned to see his kart ready in the pit lane, Konstantin already fiddling with the tires, checking the kart's performance as always. Seb slipped into his seat and gripped the steering wheel, his heart pounding not from nerves, but from sheer excitement and anticipation. He'd faced ups and downs this season—there were highs, like podium finishes, and lows, like the races where mechanical failures had left him watching from the sidelines. But through it all, he'd gotten stronger, faster, and more determined.

"Focus on the race ahead," Seb reminded himself quietly as he fitted his gloves.

Race 1: The WSK Super Cup at Franciacorta

Seb had qualified well for the WSK Super Cup at Franciacorta, and he had had strong results in the heats and pre-final. As he sat in the kart, waiting for the final to start, he felt that familiar rush of energy. The paddock was buzzing with the intensity of international racing, but Seb was no stranger to that now. The racers here were aggressive, each battle hard-fought, and he had learned how to navigate it all, one corner at a time.

Konstantin, his mechanic who had been there with Seb all year, offered him a reassuring nod from the sidelines. "Stay smart, Seb," his mom had told him that morning. "You don't need to win every battle."

Seb knew she was right. Patience, steady focus—that's what got results. But as he glanced over at the competitor next to him, the familiar spark ignited, a fire that didn't care much for patience. He could feel it building in his chest, that electric pulse that came every time he knew a win was within reach.

He was starting from position two, not the best spot with the outside line working against him. Sure enough, he'd dropped to fourth right off the start, frustration biting at him, but he hadn't let it slow him down. Each turn, each push on the straight, he'd inched closer, his mind a blur of strategy and adrenaline. Now, with only a few laps to go, he'd clawed his way back to second, his sights locked on the leader just ahead.

The gap between them was closing. He could almost taste the victory, feel the weight of it on his shoulders like a promise. "This is it," he thought, gripping the wheel tighter, heart pounding with that stubborn, unrelenting belief.

He pushed hard, closing the gap, and in turn two, seized his chance, overtaking with a clean, sharp move. He held the lead, defending with everything he had. But the next lap, he left just enough room for the driver to slip past him again. Frustration simmered as Seb watched the kart ahead begin blocking like a wall, zigzagging down the straights, defending every possible line. Each corner was a battle, each apex a trap as the leader brake-checked him, slowing Seb down just enough to let the pack behind close in, breathing down his neck.

Seb felt the impatience clawing at him, but he kept it under control. No rash moves, he told himself. Keep calm. He probed, looking for an opening, but the defence was unyielding, every attempt met with a fierce block. When the chequered flag finally waved, Seb crossed the line in third, having lost another position in the struggle. A podium finish—especially in this field—was something to celebrate, but the taste was bittersweet. He had been so close. The win had felt within reach, but as he unclipped his helmet, a pang of frustration lingered. He could've won.

Seb climbed out of his kart and was met by Konstantin, his mechanic, whose usually stoic expression softened. "Good job. You fought hard."

Seb offered a small smile in return, knowing he needed to focus on the bigger picture. The podium was still a step forward, but deep down, he knew there were even bigger wins ahead. And he was ready for them.

Race 3: The Final Italian Championship Round at South Garda

Two weeks later, Seb found himself back at South Garda Karting, one of Italy's most iconic circuits. Just the weekend before, he'd clinched second place in the TROFEO D'AUTUNNO, another podium on Italian soil, which sent his confidence soaring. But this time, the stakes felt even higher. He was here for the final round of the Italian Championship, a race that felt like the biggest test he'd faced so far. It wasn't just about the podium this time; it was about proving himself to everyone—including his dad.

Babak had flown all the way from Australia just to be here, and every so often, Seb would catch his dad's eye from the sidelines. Babak's steady, unwavering gaze held a mix of pride and encouragement that pushed Seb to dig even deeper. Seb could feel the weight of his dad's presence settling in his chest, urging him to drive with everything he had.

But on Thursday, Seb got an unexpected surprise. Broc Feeney, a friend and Australian V8 Supercar driver Seb had admired for years, was also in Italy for a GT3 endurance race and had the day off from his own commitments. When Broc showed up at the track, Seb's face lit up. For a few hours, they soaked up the atmosphere together, sharing stories and laughter that eased some of the tension in Seb's chest. Broc watched Seb's practice laps, gave him a few pointers, and even met the team. Over lunch in the paddock, they talked about Australia, racing, and the thrill of competing overseas.

It felt surreal—and special—to have Broc's support so far from home.

Qualifying, however, brought its own challenges. The cold Italian morning didn't mesh well with Seb's new tires, and finding his rhythm proved tough. He ended up qualifying 15th on the grid, far lower than he'd expected. But Seb wasn't disheartened. If this season had taught him anything, it was that racing wasn't about where you started; it was about where you finished. He'd learned that lesson more than once—and he was ready to prove it again.

In the first heat, Seb was determined to make up for lost ground. He weaved through the pack with precision, battling his way to a second-place finish. The second heat was even better. Seb took the lead halfway through and never looked back, finishing first, putting himself in a strong position for the finals.

He wound himself starting from position two for the first final. As usual he dropped a handful of positions but pushed hard to finish second. The final race was his moment to shine. Starting from seventh now, due to the reverse grid for the top eight, Seb knew he had to make quick moves if he wanted a shot at the win. By the halfway point, he had worked his way into first place, pulling away from the field. The kart felt like an extension of himself—every corner, every straight perfectly in sync. It was a feeling of control, of mastery, that he had only begun to experience this season.

When he crossed the finish line, the scoreboard showed a three-second gap to the next driver—a decisive, hard-fought win.

As Seb pulled into the pits, he spotted his mom's face first, her expression pure pride and relief. But it was seeing his dad there, taking it all in with that quiet, proud smile that meant the most.

Seb pulled off his helmet, the cool air hitting his face as he felt the weight of it all settle on him. It wasn't just about this win; it was about proving something deeper—to himself, to everyone who'd been behind him through every high and low. He could do this. And today, he had.

Race 4: The WSK Euro Series at Sarno

The final race of Seb's five-week stint was at **Sarno** for the second and final round of the WSK Euro Series. This was one of the toughest races of the year, with both juniors and seniors qualifying together. The seniors had more horsepower, but Seb didn't let that intimidate him. He had come to expect the unexpected in this sport.

Seb's kart was flying during qualifying, and he managed to out-qualify all the senior and junior drivers, stunning everyone in the paddock, by claiming pole over all. In the first heat, Seb finished third behind two senior OKN drivers. But in the second heat, something shifted.

As Seb approached the final lap, he found himself in a tight battle with one of the senior drivers for first place. His dad had told him not to race the seniors—"Your race is with the juniors," Babak had reminded him—but in that moment, Seb couldn't help himself. He overtook the senior on the last lap, crossing the line first in his heat.

The juniors and seniors were separate in both the pre-final and the final, and Seb was unstoppable. Each lap seemed to click perfectly, like he was in complete harmony with the kart. He stretched the gap between himself and the rest of the field, ultimately winning the final by more than seven seconds. Not only had he set the fastest lap of the entire event, but the dominance of his performance was undeniable.

As he climbed out of the kart and stood on the top step of the podium, the weight of his achievement began to sink in. This wasn't just a win—it was a statement. Seb wasn't just another driver in the pack; he was proving he was a force to be reckoned with.

"REFLECTION"

T his season hadn't just been about the wins or the trophies—it had been about moments. The kind of moments that stick with you, long after the roar of the engines faded. Some of those moments had little to do with the races themselves and everything to do with the people Seb met along the way.

One of the unexpected highlights of the season was seeing a familiar face, his first-ever coach, Dave, alongside his wife, Sherry. They had flown all the way to Italy to surprise Seb and cheer him on. Seeing Dave, the man who had first taught him how to handle a kart, standing there on the other side of the world, was surreal. It didn't matter that the weekend wasn't his best. Just having Dave and Sherry there, their encouragement as unwavering as it had been in his earliest days, meant everything.

Another unforgettable moment came during one practice day, when Seb found himself face to face with **Toto Wolff**, the team principal of **Mercedes-AMG Petronas Formula One Team**.

Toto had stopped by **South Garda** with his young son, and when he approached Seb in the paddock, it felt surreal. Seb was momentarily star struck but managed to steady himself as Toto offered a few words of encouragement. Seb couldn't believe he'd just met one of the most influential figures in Formula One.

The day before, Seb had crossed paths with **Kimi Raikkonen** at **Franciacorta**. Kimi had been at the track with his son, and though Seb felt nervous, he couldn't resist asking the legendary driver for an autograph. Kimi, in his usual cool, laid-back style, signed Seb's hat with a quiet nod of approval. He didn't say much—Kimi never did—but the brief exchange was enough. **Those moments—small but significant—gave Seb a glimpse of the world he was aiming for.** Formula One wasn't just a distant dream anymore. It was becoming something tangible, something he could almost touch.

But the encounters didn't stop there. Over the course of racing in Italy, Seb also crossed paths with **Mika Häkkinen**, the two-time Formula One World Champion. Mika, who had become a familiar face at several of Seb's race weekends as his two children raced in the same class as Seb, often watched from the sidelines, quietly observing the young talent. During one particular weekend, after an especially intense race, Mika approached Seb and congratulated him on his performance. "You're doing well out there," Mika had said, his Finnish accent as sharp as ever. On another occasion, **Mika even sat with Seb on the out-grid, sharing a quiet conversation before the race**. It wasn't just the advice—though it meant the world to Seb—but the recognition. **Mika Häkkinen knew his name.** These interactions weren't just chance encounters—they were pieces of a bigger picture, moments that added fuel to Seb's drive to make it to the top.

Even more surreal was racing against a new generation of motorsport legacies. Nearly every race put him on the grid with kids from famous racing families—Charles Leclerc's cousin, Max Verstappen's cousin, and others from Formula One, NASCAR, and GT lineages. These young drivers had grown up surrounded by motorsport legends, their names carrying an unspoken legacy that Seb could feel in every tight corner and fast straight. Instead of feeling daunted, he found inspiration in the challenge. He knew his path was different—there was no family legacy or well-known name backing him. It was just him, carving out his own place, determined to prove that skill, grit, and heart could stand on their own.

The season closed with more than just podiums and trophies. Seb had finished strong, securing a second-place finish in both the Italian Championship and the WSK Euro Series, with multiple first-place trophies and podiums marking his progress. But it was the respect he'd earned that mattered most—respect from teammates, competitors, and mentors who had once been strangers. Each nod of approval, each handshake from people like Mika and Toto, felt like a step closer to his dreams.

Among those watching closely was Mr. Robazzi, owner of Tony Kart, who'd made regular visits to the Ward Racing tent, talking with Joakim and Babak after each race. By season's end, there were whispers of Seb possibly re-joining the Tony Kart team in the prestigious OKJ class next year. The thought of racing for such a renowned team was thrilling, a goal that felt closer with each encouraging word from Mr. Robazzi. It reminded Babak of advice Joakim had shared earlier: "No matter how much money someone has, if they want to go far in motorsport, they need people who believe in them and are willing to help."

Those words echoed in Babak's mind every time he thought about the mentors and supporters who had entered their lives—from Tom in Toowoomba to Pete, Alessandro, Konstantin, Rebecca, and Ian. These people weren't just part of Seb's racing career; they were part of his journey, shaping him, supporting him, and believing in him as much as he believed in himself.

As Seb packed up his gear for the last time this season, a mix of pride and bittersweet emotions filled him. There were moments of triumph—standing on the podium at Sarno, celebrating a hard-won victory. But there had also been frustrating races, like the one at Franciacorta, where a win had slipped away in the final laps. Each podium, each lesson in resilience, had edged him closer to his dream of Formula One, a dream that felt more tangible with each passing season.

Sitting by the airplane window, he watched Italy disappear beneath the clouds, feeling a new sense of purpose swell within him. Italy had tested him, shaped him and shown him just how much he was capable of enduring and achieving. And now, he felt ready to face whatever lay ahead with even greater determination.

A couple of weeks later, back home in Queensland, Seb was driving back from his aunt's house, a rare break from the constant schedule of racing. As he thought back over the season, he felt a wave of gratitude for the people who had stood by him, believed in him, and pushed him to be his best. Without thinking, he pulled out his phone and sent a quick message to Konstantin. "Ciao Konstantin. Thank you for all your hard work this year. We may not have gotten all the results, but I learned so much because of you. I'm grateful for that, and I look forward to seeing what you're up to."

Moments later, Konstantin's reply came through. "Hi, my friend. Thank you for giving me so many emotions this season. It was great, and I hope you'll keep going on your way to the top. It was a beautiful time. Thanks a lot."

Seb smiled, feeling the warmth of those words sink in. This season had been about more than racing—it had been about the people, the connections and the shared belief in something bigger. With the journey to Formula One now more real than ever, he knew he was ready to chase it with everything he had, strengthened by the support of those who'd been by his side every step of the way.

Seb leaned back in his chair that evening, the warm Queensland sky glowing like the embers of a fire, much like the one burning in his chest. This season had been the proving ground, where dreams stopped feeling like fantasies and started feeling like reality. But let's be honest—this was only the first chapter of a much bigger story. The world of motorsport is ruthless, the road to Formula One even more so. Yet with every lap, every podium and every setback he'd turned into fuel, Seb knew one thing for sure: he wasn't here to play it safe, and neither were his mum and dad. The next race, the next season, the next challenge—they weren't just steps on the journey; they were the fireworks waiting to be lit. And trust me, if you thought this season was exciting, you've seen nothing yet. Tomorrow, the engines will roar, and Sebastian will be back, ready to chase the dream with a grin and a wheel-spin. Buckle up.